Matt Bernstein Sycamo[re]
Editor

Tricks and Treats
Sex Workers Write
About Their Clients

Pre-publication
REVIEWS,
COMMENTARIES,
EVALUATIONS . . .

"**O**migod, is this a delicious book or what!? *Tricks and Treats* is a painfully tantalizing must-read for every serious student of sex and gender, every feminist who's interested in the good girl/bad girl debate, and everyone who's ever harbored the secret longing to be a sex worker."

Kate Bornstein
Author, *My Gender Workbook,*
New York, NY

"**F**iercely alive with attitude, candor, and dish, *Tricks and Treats* delivers everything you were afraid to find out about sex work and more. Matt Bernstein Sycamore

has artfully assembled an intimate and uncompromising collection that reads like a revealing chat between an extended family of friends. At times scathingly humorous, at times strikingly dark, *Tricks and Treats* pulls no punches and is full of surprises. A valuable and overdue addition to the discussion of sex work, it is also a riveting collection of gifted writers and storytellers. If you're looking for cheap melodrama, self-pity, or shallow titillation, go turn on a talk show. This is the real deal told by those tough and savvy enough to pull it off."

D. Travers Scott
Author, *Execution, Texas: 1987*
and Editor, *Strategic Sex:*
Why They Won't Keep It
in the Bedroom

More pre-publication
REVIEWS, COMMENTARIES, EVALUATIONS . . .

"**I** used to say that someone who has never been a sex worker could never understand what 'the life' is truly like. Well, this brilliant book proves me wrong. I highly recommend it. A fantastic collection of stories by a remarkable group of people. I was blown away.

If you want to know what it's like to be a whore, this book gives you the experience. It's so authentic and so well written that I felt like I was back in the biz. *Tricks* is a treat. Thanks Matt. Excellent entertainment and an important document.

Someone please make this book into a Hollywood movie! It's got drama, depth, humor, great characters, love, pain, political and spiritual messages, and of course plenty of sex. The first book of its kind."

Annie Sprinkle
Prostitute/Porn Star
turned Sex Guru/Artist

"**O**n its face, this book is about the demand side of the sex for money exchange, but it is also about the conditions in which that exchange takes place. From the very first pages, the reader is forced to confront the fear of arrest while working in an underground, illegal market. The next trick could be a cop and the next time you agree to perform some sexual service in exchange for money (or, as the California law reads, "other consideration"), you could go to jail. Your closet could be forced open, and you could be subjected to relentless verbal abuse, reflective of society's condemnation of you. It is amazing, in this dangerous context, that so many sex workers are able to articulate their sense of themselves as healers, or reflect on the way clients expect them to be experts. On the other hand, it is not surprising that there are so many 'war stories,' descriptions of the unique and sometimes disturbing clients among the mostly banal. Some of the contributions seem not to be about sex work, but in fact they are, as in Jo Anne C. Heen's description of her work as a clerk in a porn video store, or Isadora Stein's of her role on an AIDS education hotline, or David Porter's on his work providing sperm for a sperm bank. Several of the writers talk about the difference between who they are and the roles they play with clients. All in all, this book takes you into a space where sex workers talk to themselves, only this time they are talking to us, the outsiders. It is an important part of a growing series of books in which prostitutes and other sex workers have projected their own voices, under their own control. Thank you, Matt Bernstein Sycamore, for bringing these voices together."

Priscilla Alexander
Co-Editor, *Sex Work: Writings by Women in the Sex Industry;*
Co-Coordinator, North American Task Force on Prostitution, New York, NY

Tricks and Treats
*Sex Workers Write
About Their Clients*

HAWORTH Gay & Lesbian Studies
John P. De Cecco, PhD
Editor in Chief

Tricks and Treats
Sex Workers Write About Their Clients

Matt Bernstein Sycamore
Editor

Harrington Park Press
An Imprint of The Haworth Press, Inc.
New York • London • Oxford

Published by

Harrington Park Press, an imprint of The Haworth Press, Inc., 10 Alice Street, Binghamton, NY 13904-1580

Cover design by Monica Seifert.

Cover photo © Michele Serchuk 1999/photodiva.com.

The Library of Congress has cataloged the hardcover edition of this book as:

Tricks and treats : sex workers write about their clients / Matt Bernstein Sycamore, editor.
    p. cm.
  ISBN 0-7890-0703-7 (hd)
    1. Prostitutes' customers—Case studies. 2. Prostitutes—Case studies. 3. Prostitution—Case studies. I. Sycamore, Matt Bernstein.
HQ117.T75 2000
306.74—dc21   CIP
                                                                                          99-056778

ISBN 1-56023-162-9 (pbk.)

To Steve Zeeland,
without whom this book might never have happened

For JoAnne (1974-1995)

ABOUT THE EDITOR

Matt Bernstein Sycamore is a widely published author and editor, an activist, and a whore currently living in New York City. He has been involved in the sex industry since age nineteen—starting in San Francisco, then continuing in Boston, Seattle, and New York—mostly as a callboy, but also as a stripper, a bodyworker, a street hustler, and a porn model.

Dedicated to direct-action street activism, Mr. Sycamore has been involved in numerous struggles for social and political change, including the fight against police brutality; AIDS activism; and a queer activism that focuses on fighting racism, classism, misogyny, and heterosexism. He has used his experience as a political organizer to compile *Tricks and Treats: Sex Workers Write About Their Clients.* Mr. Sycamore's writing has appeared in numerous publications, including *Best American Gay Fiction 3, Best Gay Erotica 2000, Obsessed, Flesh and the Word 4, The James White Review, Queer View Mirror* (volumes one and two), *LGNY, Harrington Gay Men's Quarterly Fiction* (The Haworth Press, Inc.), *Quickies, Black Sheets,* and *Women and Performance,* among others.

CONTENTS

Acknowledgments

Thanks to everyone who helped in the creation of this book, especially (in alphabetical order) Norma Jean Almodovar, Priscilla Alexander, Jean Bergman and everyone at NYPAEC, Barbara Carrellas, Johanna Fateman, Cindra Feuer, Alex Gerber, Karen Green, Jenny Ho, James Johnstone, Ananda LaVita, Michael Lowenthal, D. Travers Scott, Jason Sellards, Laurie Sirois, Greg Spector, Eve Stotland, Donald Suggs and everyone at FROST'D, Tristan Taormino, Karen X. Tulchinsky, Eric Von Stein, Stephen Winter, and anyone else whom I may have inadvertently forgotten.

To the radical activists who keep me going, and to my chosen family, especially Andee, Chrissie, Gabby, Jon, Lauren, Rebecca, Robin, Rue, zee.

To whores everywhere.

Tricks and Treats: An Introduction

My first published story, "How I Got These Shorts," starts like this:

> It's my fifth trick. He calls around eleven, says do you go to Concord. I say a hundred an hour, two-fifty for the night, wash up, catch the last train, and of course he isn't there. So I'm standing there waiting, thinking he's not going to show up and there isn't another train 'til morning and what the fuck am I going to do. Finally, this man comes up in Speedos and a windbreaker, says are you Tyler like there's anyone else around with pink hair. Then we're driving along, he's pushing my head to his crotch saying *suck my cock suck my cock* and I'm sucking his limp dick, he's doing Rush every few minutes and squeezing my balls and we're driving in the pitch dark—I don't know *where the fuck* we are. Tells me he's been up all weekend on crystal, met these two straightboys and don't I want to fuck those straightboys. I say yeah, I really want to fuck those straightboys. Says he gave the straightboys his Mercedes and they're going to show up at his house, I'm thinking hell yeah the straightboys are going to show up with your Mercedes.

And the story ends like this:

> I'm spacing out in the mirror and the straightboy comes in, looks both ways, locks the door and says shh. . . . Takes out his

"How I Got My Shorts" was originally published in *Queer View Mirror,* edited by James C. Johnstone and Karen X. Tulchinsky (Milford, CT: Arsenal Pulp Press, 1995), pp. 257-258. The story was reprinted in *Flesh and the Word No. 4,* edited by Michael Lowenthal (New York: Penguin, 1997), pp. 156-163.

cock and pretends he's gonna piss, starts jerking off. So I help
him. He comes twice, says keep this between us okay. I say
don't worry *honey*, go into the bedroom and the trick says did
you make any progress with the straightboys. I say I just
jerked one off. The other whore is trying on all this underwear,
it's like everything from the *International Male* catalog and
more. He's trying on this leopard print metallic thong, swing-
ing his hips in front of the mirror, saying things like shhh*wank*.
And that's when I put on these shorts.

In between the beginning and the end of the story, I do ecstasy at
the trick's house; make cocktails for a straightboy and suck his dick
(but then he turns out to be another whore); do more drugs; and hide
from the trick. The funniest part actually happens after the story's
end, after I get the shorts, but before I wear the shorts to perform
"How I Got These Shorts." Seven a.m. comes around and the trick
says he has to go see his patients (he's a psychiatrist), and then
somehow I end up with a check for a hundred dollars. Now, don't
ask me how I end up with—first of all—a check and—second of
all—only a hundred dollars.

All this goes to prove that every trick is just desperate to become
a story. Sometimes the story is the arrangement of toiletries in the
bathroom, and sometimes it's the trick running into the hallway in
his underwear, but, trust me, there's a story going on every time.
Originally, I would tell friends about my tricks, but I didn't see
these tales as fit for "writing." Thankfully, my friends thought
otherwise, and I'm especially grateful to Andy Slaght, who consistently reminds me that it was he who told me I needed to write down
the story about my fifth trick. In fact, "How I Got These Shorts"
was the first piece I ever wrote directly about my life. I wrote the
story just like I told it to my friends and to my journal, a casual
conversation piece.

In spite of (or perhaps because of) the fact that everything in
"How I Got These Shorts" was true, it was first published as fiction.
Most people thought that it was too outrageous to be true, at least
not all of it. I laughed when people asked which parts were true—
any of it? Clearly, these people had never met a whore because
everyone knows that a whore has stories.

Sex workers tell one another our stories—it's our form of history, our way of remembering (or forgetting), our way to communicate. When we talk to one another—or to our friends—we don't explain ourselves; we just go with it. That's what I did with "How I Got These Shorts": I forced the reader to enter the story on my terms. There's no translation, no play-by-play explication.

I put together this anthology, *Tricks and Treats: Sex Workers Write About Their Clients*, to compile the tales of other sex workers, *on our own terms*. You will find very little explanation; these stories are written as if we are talking among ourselves. This is a window into sex workers' lives, *as we see them*, and a window from our lives into the lives of the people we encounter.

This anthology takes sex work as a given, a vantage point from which to view tricks, the sex industry, and society as a whole. This is not the pathologized, sensationalized, or glamorized version of sex work that we usually see perpetuated by outsiders in the media. This is sex workers taking charge of the scrutiny.

Sex workers are sick and tired of being analyzed and abused by tricks, therapists and social workers, talk show hosts and evangelists, politicians and policemen. In this book, sex workers turn our attention to the outsiders who endlessly rework our lives in the public eye. This is our turn to shift the gaze, to put tricks under the microscope.

Priscilla Alexander, not a sex worker herself, but a renowned academic on sex work issues, once said to me, jokingly, that she didn't know anyone who wasn't a sex worker, that she just wasn't interested in anyone but sex workers. For me, it seems as if every few weeks another friend enters or reenters the sex industry in one form or another; sometimes this overwhelms me. I remember one time I had to throw a certain friend out of my car because he was making shady comments about street workers. The next week, he was on the block. Whenever another friend starts doing sex work, I ask myself whether that person is ready. Was I ready? Is anyone ever ready?

Sex workers must constantly negotiate the perilous intersections between sex, power, money, intimacy, and all the other grand issues that are intertwined in everybody's lives. But for sex workers, this is our livelihood, so we develop a unique way of looking at the world, a critical distance that can't be imitated. Our gazes instantly deconstruct. Sure, our clothes, our mannerisms, and our culture can be commodified and reproduced as lifeless accessories for the relentlessly chic, but our gazes aren't something you can buy at the Gucci boutique.

In some ways, it surprises me that this is the first book to focus specifically on clients rather than sex workers. However, our clients generally hold access to the power mechanisms that keep their identities (as the purchasers of sex services) hidden. In a world that deeply stigmatizes sex workers, clients cannot freely reveal their identities without fear of repercussions. But, just as one cannot analyze race without examining whiteness, the unquestioned (and often invisible) construct that underlies race, one cannot fully analyze sex work without looking at tricks. This book seeks to open up the shades, the locked doors, the gated subdivisions that hide the identities of the buyers of sex.

People are generally too busy gaping at the hookers to scrutinize the tricks, but sex workers do it all the time. We share tips and warnings, we bitch about the scammers, we brag and complain about our earnings, and we laugh and cry about the crazies. This anthology moves these conversations into the public domain. Here, sex workers reveal our commercial, cultural, emotional, sexual, (il)legal, and even spiritual relationships with our tricks. We take out our flashlights and illuminate them. Camera's ready; prepare to flash.

I didn't conceive of this book, however, only to further the study of sex work. Just as important, I wanted to read the stories of other sex workers to see if anyone else had their tricks figured out. Because, in five years of turning tricks, I still don't understand my tricks. It's likely that I'll always have questions. Why the hell don't I get enough regulars? Or, when I do get regulars, how come they always have to be the tricks I can't stand? Every sex worker has a formula, a worldview that explains everything, a worldview that is constantly collapsing and reforming. I embarked on this project to try to figure out my tricks (though I still haven't).

I include as broad as possible a selection of sex workers in this book: street workers, escorts, strippers, porn actors, masseurs, dominatrixes, a phone sex operator—even a video store clerk, an outreach worker, a sex educator, and a sperm donor. This book includes stories by male, female, and transgendered sex workers from different backgrounds in terms of race, class, gender, education, origin, and sexuality. Sometimes these differing backgrounds prevent sex workers from exploring our commonalities and our differences. Here, all types of sex workers tell our stories, side by side. We are an extremely diverse group, but our stories demonstrate a shared culture.

In the marketing of nonfiction anthologies, different genders are often treated as different species. I don't know of any other book that includes male, female, and transgendered sex workers. There are several good books on female sex workers, especially *Whores and Other Feminists*, edited by Jill Nagle, and the groundbreaking *Sex Work*, edited by Priscilla Alexander and Frederique Delacoste. In *Whore Carnival*, Shannon Bell interviews female—and a few male—sex workers and manages successfully to collapse the boundaries between interviewer and interviewee, making her book especially entertaining. And *WHOREZINE*, edited by Vic St. Blaise, is an indispensable collection of dish, dirt, and news.

As far as books on male sex workers, there isn't one I've found satisfying. John Preston's *Hustling* is a useful how-to book, though it only focuses on escorts. In books about sex work, transgendered sex workers are usually either ignored entirely or placed uncomfortably alongside male sex workers. A book that fully explores transgendered sex workers' lives rather than fetishizing or pathologizing the trans or sex work aspects is sorely needed.

Tricks and Treats enforces no hierarchies among the different types of sex workers. I make no attempt to decide who the "real" sex workers are (i.e., Is someone who offers his or her body for a fuck more or less of a sex worker than someone who coos a client to orgasm over the phone?). In my call for submissions, I encouraged contributors to think of the categories of "sex work" and "trick" in the broadest possible manner. Thankfully, I received several submissions that expanded my definition of sex work. In "The Porn Queen," Jo Anne C. Heen writes about how the customers at the adult video store, where she worked behind the counter, treated her like a whore. In "Payment by Donation: Every Sperm Is Sacred,"

David Porter writes about one of the newest forms of sex work: sperm donation.

We've all got our stories. I can talk about the trick who convinced me to share an entire bottle of tequila with him, tried to stick a hundred dollar bill up my ass, and then took it back when I went to the bathroom. I can tell you about the trick I stole a hundred dollars from, who then tipped me another hundred, or the trick who left me in a gated beach community while he went to work. There's the trick who actually succeeded in seducing me, reactivating my senses when I felt shut down. Then there was the trick who called six times to ask for directions, once from outside my door, but never showed up. I can tell you about the trick who gave me rectal gonorrhea when he took the condom off without my knowing. One trick kneeled by a piano bench, got hard, and then asked me to stand on his dick with all my weight, wearing combat boots. I can tell you about the trick who just wanted to kiss, for fifteen minutes, then said thank you and left.

In five years of turning tricks, I've certainly had my ups and downs. One day, I feel completely trapped, I'm broke, everyone who pages me is a scammer, and the one trick I finally get smells like dog food, treats me like a hole in the wall, and tells me I charge too much. Three days later, I've paid rent and bought a new stereo, and I'm ready for anything. Most days, it's somewhere in between. At its best, sex work offers me the opportunity to structure my life as close to my own terms as possible. People say it's the crudest capitalist transaction, but it also enables me to escape the drudgery of a dead-end job and a nine-to-five schedule.

Obviously, the media's most common portrayals of sex workers are of sex-crazed perverts or trapped victims. Sex workers struggle to counter these stereotypes, and in recent years, a number of high-profile, sex-positive sex workers have begun to publicly affirm the many virtues of sex work. In a world that still views sex workers primarily as vectors of disease (literally and figuratively), this counternarrative is crucial. Sometimes, however, sex worker spokespersons end up oversimplifying sex work by showing only the positive sides; to me, this is as inaccurate as the talk show hosts and the social workers who call us depraved or deprived. To honor and respect ourselves, we must tell all sides of the story.

In soliciting contributions to this anthology, I sent the call for submissions to hundreds of newspapers, magazines, newsletters, community centers, health care providers, and advocacy organizations in the United States and abroad. I sent the call to numerous sex work-related Web sites. I posted the call on bulletin boards across the United States. I interviewed several people and contacted a number of sex workers whom I respect and admire, both personal friends and public figures.

I ended up with twenty-four unique stories. Porn star and registered nurse Nina Hartley offers her perspective on sex work as a healing art. Sex academic Carol Queen presents a "taxonomy of tricks." Vernon Maulsby writes about realizing his/her transgendered identity when a client changed into a dress. Eva Pendleton writes about a rabbi who likes to be dominated. Jill Nagle arranges a trick for herself (and three boy whores) in a boy hustling bar. Scott O'Hara describes getting high from being ogled. Tony Valenzuela writes about being an HIV-positive porn-star prostitute and trying to date. Brian Pera recounts how a brothel became more of a home for him than his family of origin.

This book consists of twenty-four stories that resonated for me. Though I have attempted to include stories by as diverse a group of sex workers as possible, surely I've left many out. Every day, I hear new stories. I do not mean this book to be representative of all sex workers, but rather to exist as a collection of individual, compelling narratives of specific lives. However, in many ways, the more intensely personal a story feels, the more it represents. I've organized the stories into three categories: *tricks, treats,* and *tricks and treats.* Keep in mind that many of the stories could have gone in at least two, or even all three, of the categories. And, of course, one whore's trick is another whore's treat.

For sex workers, this book exists as a testament to our lives, a manifestation of our spirit, and a chance to turn the tables on our clients. For outsiders, this book offers a glimpse into the minds of sex workers and a spotlight on our clientele. And for tricks: well, here's what we *really* think.

TRICKS

– 1 –

Shut Up

Ann Renee

Longshoreman

He's lonely, he says. Rich and lonely. Big, hulky kinda guy, dressed sloppily in a shirt without a tie. Sloppily, he comes up to me at the fancy filigreed bar, talking low and fast and seamless. He's a seedy kinda guy, talking seamless.

"I'm so lonely. My wife died just last month." He puts his drink down next to mine and rubs his finger along the stem of my glass. I gulp my Johnny Walker and look at his shoes.

"I'm a longshoreman," he continues, without prompting. "Just here for the weekend. I'm lonely—lots of money and nothing to do."

Something's seedy here; this guy's a portfolio trick, a textbook john. Easy bait I'm supposed to swallow whole. Swallow whole and tough, not chewing. I look at his shoes.

I look at his shoes, cuz I hear Johnny inside. You can always tell a cop by his shoes, baby. Just look at those clumsy black shoes.

So I'm not biting or chewing, and he is pushing his textbook lines and starts to get huffy, challenging me. "What's in your briefcase?"

"My poetry and a book on metaphysical art."

"Oh yeah?" He snorts slightly and leans back on his elbow.

"Yeah." I pull out my book. "Do you know De Chirico's work? His paintings have really inspired my writing. I love his use of the architectonic design as a means of making the space potent and the form empty." I open the book to one of my favorite paintings. "Have you seen his work? Check this out."

He looks blankly at me. No responses prepared. He clears his throat and huffs out an exhale.

I smile. "Well, gotta go." I gather my things, touch his sleeve. "Sorry about your wife."

Out in the street, I hear big, black shoes clacking clumsily behind me. I slip down to the subway and lose him in the crowd.

Little Black Book

I swallow some wine down. Something's off today. Something's strange as I park the car. Something's strange. But I'm back. I'm back in the Copley Plaza lounge again after more than a year with a little black book and lists of men. Lists of men looking to be my slave, looking to lick my boots. Looking to pay me a hundred or more for a few chains and rationed touch. I'm not back here to lay up in their rooms. I'm here because this time I'm going to do it right. I don't want to be touched by the cops or the johns or the bartenders, so I'm screening these guys with public interviews in this classy café. Screening these guys to choose the few special ones.

My 12:45 p.m. appointment approaches, wearing the blue striped shirt as described. "Alexa?" He approaches hesitantly, scans his eyes to my boots. "Alexa?" I nod and swoop my head slightly to indicate his seat. I check my book: #33, 12:45 p.m., Wally, blue striped shirt.

"You must be Wally?"

He moves his slight body around in the wide chair, unable to find the right spot. I lower my chin and fix my eyes on him. "Tell me what you like, Wally."

He shifts around again, then leans forward, rolling the napkin and absently rubbing his fingers along the Copley Plaza Logo.

"Wh—what do you mean?"

I lean back, exhale. "You know what I mean, Wally."

His forehead begins to shine with sweat. "I, I don't like pain, only light whips."

I nod, write "lght whps" beneath his name.

"What arc you writing?" He looks around the empty foyer bar, up to the elaborate vaulted ceiling, and then back at me.

"Just notes to remember you by. Go on, Wally."

"I don't like—I don't like dresses."

I jot down "no tv" and look up with mock impatience.

"I want to—I like toilet training."

"Water sports?" I ask.

"Yes, and . . ."

"And?" I ask him directly and calmly, as if I'm asking him what cocktail he prefers.

He blurts out, "And shit too. Do you do that? Will you?" I jot down "eats shit" as Wally drops his head, twisting his napkin around his index finger.

When I look up from my book, I see two men behind Wally at the opposite table. They are a mismatched pair. One is a well-dressed black man with an overcoat and silk scarf. The other one is white, dressed sloppily in a shirt without a tie. He's got big black cop shoes. I recognize him. Two years ago, same beat. This is the cop who tried to frame me while posing as a longshoreman. The two have caught my eye and are making a poor theater of indifference.

Fuck, I think, acting unaffected. "Wally, I'll be contacting you." I hold out my hand for the twenty-dollar interview fee.

"Is your apartment nearby?" he asks, as he fumbles through his wallet.

"I'll let you know." I remain cool and matter-of-fact, my mind frantic.

"Look, Wally," I say and lean forward. "If someone asks you what we were talking about, tell them . . . tell them I was interviewing you for my thesis on art history."

I have no idea if Wally has a clue about art history. Terror bonds up poor Wally's throat. "Why should anyone ask?"

I'm genuinely sorry he has to be subjected to this. "Don't look behind you, but I believe the two men sitting there are cops."

Wally sinks back in his chair. "Wh—what should I do?" He grips the arms of his chair, confused, utterly deflated. I'm sorry for his terror, but I'm impatient that he can't meet the intervention with more calm. I'm a stranger, I remind myself, and he's just told me he likes to eat shit.

Finally, Wally gets up stiffly and walks out the door. The "long-shoreman" quickly and clumsily rises and follows him. The other man with the silk scarf walks up to me and spreads his leather badge carrier in front of my face. "Police. You're under arrest."

Godammit, I think. "Why?" I respond with indignant surprise.

"Didn't you just take money from that man?"

"So now it's illegal to take money from someone?"

He doesn't respond.

"You're under arrest. Give me your purse." He goes through my purse and wallet. He picks up the black book. I hold my breath. He puts it down.

Longshoreman comes back into the lobby.

"Cuff her," he says, triumphantly. "She propositioned him."

"That's a fucking lie!"

"Come on, get up." The scarved one holds my elbow. I stand up. They cuff me. Then, flanking either side of me, they proudly parade me through the entire lobby, their slave for the afternoon.

Shut Up

You can always tell a cop by his shoes, baby. Just look at his clumsy black shoes. Johnny knows. Johnny's caramel lips would tell me. Look out for those black shoes.

But this time I didn't catch the shoes in time. They've got my purse with the black book in it, and I'm shut up in this cell, being held.

"One call. You got one call, honey." The cop, indifferent as a waitress on her twelfth hour, unlocks my cell, points his ink-stained index at the phone. One call, one call. I dial Jack's beeper cuz he's got cash and he'll know what to do. "Will. It's Alexa. I've been arrested. Fifth precinct."

There's an excited raising of voices behind me. One of the cops grabs my arm from behind. "She just used a pseudonym, Joey; let's book her." He looks at me, still holding my elbow, speaking slow and labored. "You just used a pseudonym, girl!"

I don't respond. He shoves me back into the holding cell. I sit on the bench, leaning against the side wall, staring at the opposite wall, legs and arms crossed.

"A pervert!" The cops are now passing my black book back and forth between each other, reading, smirking, and then looking over at me. I stare ahead blankly, pretending to be unaffected as they read. Which client profile are they reading about now, I wonder?

"# 25, 10 a.m., Eric, blue shirt, whps, chains, tv, no pierce?"

"#29, 2 p.m., Clyde, tv, no marks, blk stockngs?" Have they realized yet that the man who says I propositioned him was "# 33, 12:45 p.m., Wally, blue striped shirt, lght whps, no tv, ropes, no chains, eats shit"?

One cop comes to eye me. He paces back and forth in front of my cell, amused. "A pervert. We have a sexual pervert locked up here."

"Fuck off," I say, still staring at the opposite wall.

"Well, she's definitely getting shut up in the women's jail now!"

I stay mute, expressionless, waiting in this cell. The air is hot and thick, smells like boots, black boots.

"Hey," a soft, patronizing voice calls to me. "Hey, man, how are you?" Here's a soft-talking, plain-clothed man dressed in jeans and a corduroy jacket. The one with the Velveeta voice. The one that studied psychology as his cop training. The one who's learned how to get me to talk. The one who's supposed to get me to talk is talking to me now.

"Hey, man." He makes these bread-dough eyes at me. "It really hurts me to see you locked up inside there like this."

I cross my five-inch-heeled boot the other direction and recross my arms, turning from the wall to look out the bars at him. "It really hurts me to see you out there."

"So, why did you use a pseudonym? Who's Will? It will be easier for you if we know who Will is." He pauses strategically. I push my back tighter against the cold cement wall and continue staring ahead. I remember Johnny telling me, "They'll make you talk, Alexa. They'll try to make you talk. So don't talk. Whatever you do, don't talk."

I'm good at not talking. I can shut up and stay shut up. I've stayed shut up about some things for years. So I can sit here with Mr. Persuasion. I can sit here with Mr. Velveeta Voice in this cell smelling like black boots. I can sit here and not say a thing.

Bang the Pipes

The cops have little patience for lying perverts. They take me on a handcuffed paddy wagon ride to the women's jail. From one jail to the next, a blind drive.

"Get out." The female cop unlocks the wagon, grabs my arm, and sneers at me, up and down.

She looks at me like I'm sleaze, and she greases up my fingers and prints me and sets me in the photo cell to mug me front and side.

Lady cop takes me upstairs to the cells. "Take off those boots." I take them off. She rips out the lining. "Fred, will ya just look at what they spend their money on." Tosses the one boot on the floor and goes for the other one. "Take off your dress." Standing there with lady cop and Fred watching, I undress. She puts her hand down my underwear.

"You're lucky you're clean this time. Next time you won't be so lucky."

They shove me into the piss-covered cell. I wait. Does anyone know I'm in here? Did Will get the call?

"Hey, honey." A drawling voice calls to me from the adjacent cell. "Hoannny? You hear me? Wha'syer name?"

"Ann. M'name's Ann."

"Bradie, here. I'm dyin' fera cigarette. Damn. Been in here all day. Hey, hey!" She starts banging the toilet pipes. "Let's bang the pipes. Bang the pipes, Annie, so's we can have a smoke. C'mon, Annie, bang the pipes."

"Bradie?"

She keeps banging.

"Bradie, I don't want any more bullshit than I already got."

"Hey! Hey coppers! C'mere—I want a smoke!"

A cop yells through the outside bars, "Shut up, Bradie!"

Bradie mumbles for a while and then says, "Whatchu in here fer, Annie?"

"Prostitution."

"Hah. All the good time folk're locked up tonight."

"Yeah. Good time folk, that's right," I say.

Hours later, Will brings the bail. He's not talking. Back home, he's bothered. I'm crying and he doesn't want me to bug him. He pushes me over to my side of the bed.

"Get over it," he tells me, turning to face the wall. "You weren't even in overnight."

Gray Flannel

My lawyer's gonna clear this up. Tells me I have a strange case. It's not illegal to make plans to whip a consenting adult. There's not even a law on the books about eating feces. He tells me to buy a gray suit and get a job. In an insurance company, he says. Something like that, really straight.

So I buy squared-off pumps and a gray flannel suit and I get hired the next week at American International. High-risk insurance. Kidnap and ransom, bombs, and satellites.

I walk in my suit to City Hall, the hall of justice and piss and musty books of law. I find the courtroom where I'm to be tried with the other hookers and transvestites who all know one another. It's a family thing—getting arrested every few days.

The silk-scarfed officer who arrested me approaches. "We've never had a case come up like this before. In fact, I don't know if the witness will show."

I laugh. "That man Wally? Probably not. You know, I didn't proposition him. In fact, he didn't want to get fucked at all."

"Yeah, I know; we figured that. That little black book—" He tilts his head to one side. "What are you really doing in this business? You don't have to tell me, but what else do you do in your life?" He shakes his head and can't understand why I'm here.

"I don't want to see you convicted," he says. "I'll see what I can do."

My lawyer escorts me into the courtroom. We sit down, waiting in the pews of the law. Finally, we're called to the bench; the arresting cop comes up, and the judge says some convoluted verbiage meant to obscure truth—something about "insufficient evidence." We leave.

"Have to come back next week." My lawyer says. "They get three times to come up with evidence."

Next week, we come to City Hall. We sit, wait, and leave. Insufficient evidence.

The following week I come to the great hall of the city. My lawyer comes in the courtroom, looking concerned. He leans over to me, touches my arm. "Wait here. There may be trouble." He goes outside for a while.

My gray flannel's sticky. I recognize a wigless transvestite with shaved eyebrows. He winks at me and says, "In here again, honey? You know," he waves his long-ringed hand by his face, "I just want to go up to the bench and say, 'Yes, Mr. I Judge Your Honor, I did suck him off, and it was gooood!'" A number of us chuckle.

My lawyer comes back, smiling. "Let's go, Ann. You're free."

He loops his arm through mine as we walk out. "Whatever you do," he warns, "don't look to the left."

Of course, I look to the left. The arresting cop sits next to the "evidence." He's sitting next to Wally. Wally, the evidence. Insufficient evidence—doesn't like whips but wants to eat shit. Wally's hunched over. Must've made a deal.

–2–

My Path to Sanity

Vernon Maulsby (Mikki)

I started making porn loops to pay off a gambling debt. I can still remember the scent of competing disinfectants that filled the air of the musty building, crammed with prop walls, lights, and strangers with dead eyes. After a few moments, I was on a double bed, my back sweating from the hot lights, and my phallus was buried deep inside some small white guy, his smelly feet against my ears. A director ordered every move from offstage. I remember the director had to tell the guy under me to get the bored look off his face.

Having to come on cue was tough—hell, just keeping it up was hard—this guy felt like his ass had no sides to it. He was a pro and was kind enough, once he saw my problem, to clamp down some. That gave me enough feeling to finally come to orgasm. Even when I came, over the guy's plain but unlined face, his eyes remained dead, as if we were on an elevator together. Once I was done, I was given a hundred in cash and pointed to a very mildewed shower stall. I was amazed to see a pan of blue disinfectant right in front of the shower, but not too shocked to use it. As I got out, my film partner went in. The stall didn't have a curtain, so I looked the guy over. When I reached his eyes, I clearly saw the distaste there and hurried into my clothes and out the door.

I was a big, hulking bear of a black man, over six feet tall, and a lot over two hundred pounds. This was the seventies, and black aggressor movies were in vogue, so I got a lot of work. The plots were generic: I would enter some little white guy's room, usually with a silly plastic gun in my hand, then I would pretend to rough him up a bit, tear off whatever prop undies he had on, and "rape" him.

19

The silliness didn't end there. Usually, I had to grab a handful of greasy hair and act like I was forcing the guy to go down on me, being careful not to come, as this would have wasted time and film. Then I always had to force the guy into a position favorable to the camera and fuck him, making it look as rough as possible by slapping his buttocks, grabbing his hair, or forcing his feet up to his (or my) ears. Finally, I was allowed to come on the guy's face or chest, depending on the director. The ultimate silliness came next, when the guy I was supposed to be abusing had to act as if he'd loved the experience, usually by kissing my lubricant-and-feces-flavored phallus.

There was some variety. I did a few outside locations, usually on rooftops, where we could film undisturbed. These had the added feature of allowing me to get even more physical, as I had to tear more clothes off the "victim," and there was the added discomfort of a gravel-topped roof, which was no good on my knees. I even did a few scenes at night, where I had to force myself on guys in an alleyway. What sticks most in my memory were the silly smiles ordered by the director at the end of these things.

I was doing drugs—I had been before I started porn loops, but now I could afford a lot more. Soon I was a real mess, of no use to anyone, and found myself out of work, homeless, and addicted to speed. My dreams of a college education were a wreck at my feet. It would be an understatement to say that I had a lot of anger within me, at everyone and everything but myself.

I wasn't much of a hooker at first. I'd go down on someone for a cigarette, if that's what I wanted at the time, or a drink or a hit or a line. I just didn't care. When I got busted by an undercover cop one night, it scared me. Instead of busting me on a sodomy rap, he just busted me for the nickel of grass in my pocket, so I suppose I was lucky. I ended up with a suspended sentence and got out of town, hoping things would change if no one knew about me and my past.

In the new town, those loops came back to haunt me. Even now, I still run into guys who think they might have seen one. The loops were so generic, so fetish bound, who can say? The same theme played over and over; the faces don't matter. Anyway, when I first moved, I ran into someone who recognized me; he was about forty, a slim, tank-topped blond with hound dog eyes. He gave great head but had an ass two people could have used at once. At least his feet were clean. When it was over, he didn't want to pay. I got pissed and roughed him up a bit. When he came, it all finally sank in, that *this* was what the guy had been trying to buy all along, my anger: a real-life example of what he'd seen in those loops. After punching him some more and seeing his phallus rise again, I took my fee out of his wallet and left him there in the hotel room. He ended up becoming my first regular.

Word traveled fast, and business began to boom for me. I loathed having to act like some big butch aggressor, having to pull punches, having to be so very careful not to leave bruises where they might be noticed, and never, never being able to be myself. My prices were reasonable, and I had enough money for shelter and my addictions, so I should have been happy, but all I felt was distaste and anger. My anger increased with every trick, every time I saw some asshole who was doing much better than I ever would be, paying me just to be hurt.

Luckily, I kept control and never hurt a trick more than he wanted. I refused to hit guys with things like whips or canes, drawing the line at a wooden ruler or a hairbrush. I also kept limits on the bondage stuff. Restraints made me ill, and a lot of easy money was lost to me because of my "scruples." I was careful, but still being eaten up inside, like each trick was a drink of acid.

Things changed when I met "Eddie," a plump guy in his midthirties. I'd seen him around, usually with the leather boys, but since I was a denim boy, we had never crossed paths. When he did hire me, I learned that he was a tv, one who came with his own gym bag full of props. Many tricks came with bags, but what was different with Eddie was what he had in the bag. Where others had smelly gym socks or underwear, Eddie had a small makeup case, a wig, some fairly sexy underwear, and a bottle of Evening in Paris, a drugstore perfume familiar to mothers for decades. Eddie went into the bathroom, bag in hand, and came out as a plump gal in high heels, seamed stockings, garter belt, bra, and the long kind of slip Sophia Loren made famous.

Eddie wanted rough sex all right, but he wanted to be dominated as a woman. This blew me away, opened my eyes up to a very hidden self-truth, that all of my life, *this* was what I had always wanted for myself. For all of the butch posturing, I wanted to be loved as a woman. It shook me up, seeing Eddie dressed as he was, in full makeup. I saw my own needs and desires mirrored in this trick. I was so in tune with his needs that the anger that had fueled my work just drained away. I had none left to sell him. I returned his money, leaving him unhappy and unabused.

3

Man of God

Eva Pendleton

He is a man with, as they say, everything to lose. He has two teenaged children, who live with their mother most of the time. He heads a modest congregation somewhere in New York City. He has a trust fund of a value that is difficult to determine, but it supports his various habits.

I see the rabbi every couple of weeks. When we first met, I would see him more often, usually a couple times a week. On that schedule he pretty much supported me throughout my first year of grad school. There's an ebb and flow to our three-year relationship, a cyclical pattern revolving around the rabbi's fantasy of what we are to each other and how close that fantasy can come to reality. We'll take several months off at a time, then we'll start seeing each other again every couple of weeks, until he becomes saturated with his feelings for me.

He gorges himself on me like I gorge myself on ice cream. Then I spend a couple of weeks forcing myself away from the aisle where they keep the Häagen-Dazs at the deli until it feels safe to eat it again. He'll call me when his hunger for me becomes greater than his fear of me. I'll call him when my hunger for cash becomes greater than my trepidation at playing the role of pusher. A pusher of kink.

I've never let the rabbi fuck me. He wants to, of course. That's part of the game. He offered me five hundred dollars to have "real sex" with him, and I refused. No matter how much he would pay me, it could never be enough; he disgusts me so. The sex we have is real enough for me: I tie him up and give it to him up the ass. He begs me to sit on his face, and I occasionally oblige, but after a few minutes, I stand up, sighing out of boredom. He makes a fool of himself for me, and I punish him for looking stupid. He tells me he loves me, and then I leave. He wants to give me pleasure, and I refuse it.

He wants to make me like him so he won't have to pay me anymore to hang out with him. I want him to pay me enough to make me like him. It's a no-win situation for both of us. Still, he pays me well when I see him. And I really don't have to do much: keep him company, look pretty, fuck him up the ass, and keep myself just out of reach.

When I see the rabbi, I dole out truths and half-truths, sometimes outright lies, depending on what I think he wants to hear. When I am with him, I become what he wants me to be: a sweet young woman; a cruel, unattainable mistress. I give him something to long for, something to want. I give him nothing.

He is a man with, as they say, everything to lose. He introduced me to his children at a street festival outside his synagogue one day, then we went inside so that he could give me the money he owed me from the previous night's session. He told me he wanted to do a scene in the temple one day, that he wanted to wear his Tallith and have me give it to him with my strap-on. We never did do that scene.

The rabbi has a number of vices; I am only one of them. About a year ago, he switched from snorting heroin to smoking cocaine. I used to feed him lines. Now I just watch as he lights up. I can't quite bring myself to hold the pipe to his lips. One evening, as I choked on the sweet stench of his secondhand smoke, I asked him whether he was ever afraid of having a heart attack from smoking: "Aren't you afraid you might OD?" I asked. He just stared blankly at me and said he'd never thought about it. He had no idea that he'd traded up on the drug risk scale, that junkies live longer than crackheads.

Most of the drug users I've known have been more or less self-reflective about it. Unlike them, the rabbi has no clue about (a) the quality of the product, (b) the fair market price, (c) the potentially harmful consequences of his behavior, and (d) the pros and cons of trusting his deepest secrets to a handful of junkies and whores. He's a fool, really—a patsy. But he's my patsy. That is, until he runs out of money. Or gets found out. Or kills himself.

The fantasy of "realness" can be the most compelling fantasy of all. It's why he keeps coming back to me. I use the "realness" of his feelings to make him fall even more deeply in love with me, or with his idea of who I am. When we first met, I pretended to be Jewish, raised in a nonreligious home. I contemplated asking him for religious instruction, spinning the initial falsehood into an elaborate, long-term deception. But I realized it would be too much work. I don't need to go that far to trigger his fantasy, just plant a little seed and let him take it from there.

Sometimes he loses track of his emotional reality. He'll convince himself that he is in love with me and that if he tries hard enough, I just might fall in love with him. He tells me this. He sings silly songs, trying to act cute. He asks me if I could ever love him. I cringe and avoid the question. He knows he's in a bind, and he tells me, "One man might fall in love with a non-Jewish woman, or with a married woman. But for me, the problem is that I have to pay you. I guess no situation is perfect, so I'll have to live with it."

For me, of course, the problem is that he resents paying me. And that it's easy to rely on the money he gives me during his binges, so that when he needs to take a break from me, I find myself broke and unable to alter my spending habits. I never want to feel so desperate for money that I lose sight of my limits. Once he called me late at night, after I was asleep. My rent was late, and I didn't know how I was going to pay it. He was high and lonely and begged me to come up and see him. I tried to let him talk me into coming over, but he wouldn't tell me what I wanted to hear: how much extra money he would pay me if I got out of bed and took a cab uptown. I almost did it anyway, but if I had, I would have felt like I was sinking down to his level. No matter what, I have to keep myself above him.

He'll tell me that he wishes I could be his girlfriend or that I could fall in love with and marry him. In my reality, the idea is so preposterous, I can hardly keep from laughing in his face: *Marry you? I can hardly stand to look at you, and the smoke from your crack pipe makes me sick to my stomach. Why on earth would I marry a crackhead rabbi? I'm a lesbian, and I'm not even Jewish.*

We've run up against the limit: we can go no further; our fantasy world and our reality world have become dangerously close. Our worlds nearly collided one day at the synagogue when I ran into an acquaintance of mine in the rabbi's office. I started to panic but somehow managed to act like my presence there was not in the least bit unusual. I started to manufacture a backup story in my head, just in case: *The rabbi's been counseling me on some problems I'm having. He's so compassionate and caring, really; I don't know what I'd do without him.* Trying to imagine a plausible scenario to cover up what's really happening, that I'm there because *he* needs *me*, not the other way around. Or that my financial need for him can be masked by a more appropriate need.

Like that shape in geometry, the hyperbola: two curves almost touch, then come to their limit, and have no choice but to veer apart. When we're together, I can manufacture the limit at the same time that I manufacture the fantasy. I pretend I'm really interested in being his girlfriend. I tell him that maybe we'll go to the movies sometime. He begins to imagine me by his side at one of his rabbi functions, a dinner or something, a pretty girl to have on his arm. Then I begin to urge him to try harder: *I'd need to be pretty secure financially to be able to do those things with you. I'm so busy; I don't really have much free time.* He begins to imagine himself as my sugar daddy, and then he freaks out and disappears on me for a few weeks.

What would it mean for him to become my sugar daddy? He'd have to give up all his other "girlfriends" because he wouldn't be able to afford them and me. (His rich catalog of vices includes several women who will have other kinds of sex with him for money.) He already has two kids that he can barely care for; he doesn't need a woman clinging to him for financial stability. And I have no business clinging to a junkie for financial stability, either. Or letting someone who repulses me even kiss me, let alone fuck me. That's my limit.

He is a man with, as they say, everything to lose. He came close to overdosing on smack once when I was with him. At least he seemed pretty close to it. He was standing in the corner of his bathroom leaning over the toilet, sweating profusely and shaking. I left him there to clean up his own mess. He doesn't even remember it happened. How many other times has he come close to losing everything?

I'm sure he gets high nearly every day. The other day, I stopped by his synagogue (his secretary knows me by name) to pick up some money he owed me. He was unshaven, rumpled, and his face looked fatigued. "How are you?" I asked. "So-so," he replied, avoiding eye contact. "How are you doing?" I asked again. "So-so, not too well." He finally looked at me, knowing that I was the only person in the synagogue who understood. "Thanks for asking." He was on his way to perform Friday evening services. I enjoy the power of knowing what's wrong with him, even though it makes me uncomfortable. Is it really power if you can't do anything with it? It's not as if I'd use it to blackmail him, though I certainly could if I wanted to. The thought of it tantalizes me and terrifies me at the same time.

He used to come over to my house in the early afternoon, get high, do a scene, and then go to work. Once he told me about a business lunch where he was so dope sick that he had to run off to the bathroom to throw up. He came back and told everyone that he had the flu. I wondered what his excuse would be to run off after services tonight, to beg off from socializing: "I'd love to, but I'm really not feeling very well. Yes, it seems to be my allergies acting up again—I just need to go home and rest." He'd get out of there as quickly as he could and run home to meet a girl (or boy) who would bring him escape.

Some of the people in his congregation suspect that he's a pot-head (which is also true, though that particular fact almost seems incidental). They tried to oust him, but the rest of the congregation rallied behind him and saved his ass. It's unthinkable to them that their beloved rabbi would ever do such a thing as smoke pot. If I told any of them that he smokes cocaine, they would laugh in my face. He'd make up a story about how he's been counseling *me* for *my* drug problem and isn't it too bad that I'm so delusional that I would accuse him, the rabbi, of such behavior. . . . It'll never happen, at least not that way. They won't find out from me.

One day he'll fall, though, and fall hard. I might be around to see it; I might not. If I am, what role will I play? Will he ask for my help? Would I give it to him if he asked? Will I even find out, or will he just disappear?

4

The Porn Queen

Jo Anne C. Heen

"How does it feel to be a purveyor of filth?" the little man asked me, in a deliberately loud voice. I usually ignored the four-foot-high dwarf, who called me "Porn Queen," and "The Madam," but it had been an especially bad day, and the video store was filled with men getting their evening smut fix. A few snickered. Instead of answering, I hit a few keys on the computer cash register, turned on the printer, and waited as it spit out six pages. I waved them in front of the man like a banner.

"Here's a list of everything you've rented in just two months." I paused. "How does it feel to spend eight hundred dollars on pornography?" I gave him my yes-I'm-a-cunt smile and watched as he crept off. I studied the sea of now-embarrassed male faces.

"Who's next?" I cooed.

I'm not quite sure how anyone can equate being a clerk in a video store with the world's oldest profession, but most of my customers did anyway. In 1990, I was the proud owner of a brand-new liberal arts degree. By 1992, after countless blue-collar minimum wage jobs, I came to the horrible conclusion that college had prepared me to do nothing. As I set off on yet another job search, I decided to take the first one that offered air-conditioning and some form of medical insurance. For a lark, I applied to work in a video store. At least I could watch movies in between waiting on customers.

I interviewed and got offered a manager position. The store rented both family fare and adult videos. Let me rephrase that. In the front of the store were about two hundred "regular" movies. They sat on the shelves, and once a week, I dusted them. What rented were the thousands of X-rated films in the back room.

My store was the smallest of six owned by a local man. All six stores carried extensive pornographic titles, although nothing approaching my store's inventory, and only mine was located in an out-of-the-way place and never advertised. Word of mouth brought in the customers, mostly men. To my surprise, they weren't the stereotypical disgusting old geezers in raincoats. There were uniformed cops and well-dressed businessmen, mechanics, and college boys, and even a few women, alone, all of whom were taking a class that required them to watch dirty movies. Everyone viewed me as some all-knowing, free-spirited, amoral sexpert provided by the company to act as mother, sister, lover, confessor, and advisor. At $4.79 an hour, I barely wanted to be the clerk.

"All he wants to do is fuck me up the ass," the young woman whispered to me. Her boyfriend was one of many in-every-day customers. He always rented one anal sex video. I had never seen the girlfriend before.

"I hate being fucked up the ass. It hurts," she continued.

"Tell him."

"He'd break up with me."

"Maybe that's best."

"I love him! We might get married. I thought you could tell me how you handle it, but you aren't very helpful." Another regular brought in his wife, pointed at me, and said, "She likes sex. She watches these movies all the time. Why can't you watch just one and try some of the stuff on it?" The wife shot me a disgusted look and walked away, while her husband asked if I'd like to come over to their house and "show her how it's done." Despite being a heavy renter, up until this incident, the man had never spoken a word to me. What was so ironic was that I really didn't know that much about sex. I liked to masturbate, enjoyed missionary position sex, and even sucked some cock, but that hardly qualified me to give advice. I found it hard to relate to the customers, who all seemed to have one thing in common, a deep obsession with the product. Customers could only rent six tapes per store a day. I don't know why—a glitch in programming, perhaps—but a rule, nonetheless. One man, a truck driver who drove a local route, found a way around this rule by stopping into each store and renting six movies at each. Every day. The owner wondered if the guy would hire on as interoffice mail boy. After I quit, I heard he applied for my job.

Despite a very diverse clientele, they all fell into what I dubbed Category One or Category Two. C1 included the customers who never spoke to me. They came in, made their selections, paid, and left. They were my favorites. C2 customers treated me like a good-time girl. Their teasing was light but lewd, often coming dangerously close to sexual harassment. They followed me from shift to shift: some were waiting for me to open in the morning; others turned up near closing and just stood around, acting like they wanted to ask for something but were too shy and hoped I'd make the first move. At times, I wanted to give in and act the way they expected me to, fuck them on the floor after closing or join them in their trash talk, but then I'd get angry and wonder what gave them the right to associate me with what I rented to them. It might be a cliché, but I learned a while ago not to let my mouth write checks my body couldn't cash because, with most men, every day is payday. I was just the clerk, the seriously underpaid, shy, white-bread clerk, and being any other way made me uncomfortable.

About a year after I was hired, the owner bought the building next door, cut a hole in the wall, and filled it with adult films. Rows and rows of girl on girl, gay male, amateurs, the scary Freaks of Nature series, big boobs, and anal videos filled the newly built shelves. The store's daily take tripled overnight, and even the customers who never spoke to me looked around in shock and guilty pleasure and began calling me Porn Queen. The men were getting ruder, and I was sick of sipping my morning coffee surrounded by twats, tits, and the nitwits who rented them. And, I was turning into the Porn Queen. I sampled the merchandise and found there were a couple of movies I really enjoyed. (I stole them when I left.) I could actually identify individual actresses. *Hustler* bought six fantasy letters I wrote and sent in.

One winter day, during the height of a fierce blizzard, I was at work, worrying about getting home. The radio was announcing school and factory closings, and several main roads were about to be shut down. Several regulars, driving big Blazers and other utility vehicles enhanced with chains for better traction, pulled into the lot at the same time the owner arrived with two cases of new rentals.

"Boy, maybe you better get home," he said, as he struggled through the door. He dropped the cases next to the counter and was immediately surrounded by a group of grown men, dressed in snowsuits, pushing and shoving to see what he had brought.

"Open it," one demanded. My boss shot me a look, and I swear I actually saw dollar signs in his eyes. I slit open the top case and bent down to pull out a handful of tapes. The men actually swarmed. I was shoved and knocked to the ground. No one apologized or helped me up. My boss asked excitedly, "How long will it take you to get them on the shelf?"

"What about the storm?" I asked.

"Oh, it's not so bad out there." Then he left, in a 4×4 with a snowplow attached. He didn't even bother to plow out the parking lot. One of the renters did.

"So what's the attraction with these films?" I finally asked a friendly regular one day. He explained that men were always on the lookout for variety.

"Say I'm screwing this woman. The sex is great. Another woman walks into the room, and, suddenly, I start wondering what it would be like with her. Maybe she sucks cock differently. Or she likes to bite and scratch and the one I'm with doesn't. Even though I'm having sex, I'm thinking of the next time." I listened to him expound on sex for over an hour and even found myself writing some stuff down.

"That's why men rent so many videos. They always hope they'll see something different. Or, if not different, at least with a different type of woman."

So there it is, for all you wannabe porn filmmakers: come up with something new and different, and the world will beat off on the path to your door.

–5–

Champagne Tastes on a Crystal Budget

Gary Rosen

Derek always said he had champagne tastes on a crystal budget. I never totally understood that—whenever he got some money, he spent it on crystal, and if he got a lot of money, he bought a lot of crystal. But still, every time Derek emptied his pockets at night while he was opening the refrigerator, turning them inside out to show what he got that day, out would pop a square Ziploc bag of crystal, along with other junk—phone numbers of new pals, appointment times for dates scrawled on a matchbook, ink-line drawings of dying bodies with pustules mushrooming out from every piece of flesh, flyers for bands, etc. Everything else was thrown on the floor next to the bed, but the crystal bag was lovingly placed in his purple velvet drawstring drug bag. The little Ziploc bag was so small and elusive that it would attach itself to other things, or stubbornly cling to the bottom of Derek's pocket, or find its way to the inside pocket of his Levi's, etc., and Derek would turn the entire room upside down, figuring that the crystal had slipped out somewhere between the door and the refrigerator, and tear his backpack apart, even though he never put drugs in his backpack cuz he was afraid someone would take 'em while he was walking down the street. "Fuck!" he'd say. "I fucking lost it at New Dawn!" Or "That fucking Eddie—he stole my fucking crystal!" But then he'd calm down when he wrenched the little pack of matte white grains out of his pocket. He'd look at me and turn his bratty-boy face around like he was trying to feign ambivalence, even though he only had three looks on his face he could successfully pull off—a really happy grin, like he'd just been fucked in the ass by an ice cream cone with sprinkles on top; a don't-fuck-with-me look that simultaneously scared off and attracted scads of people; and a puffed-out-lip look in the middle of sex, like this was the most mind-blowing experience he'd ever had. He did the last one too well and too often for it to be real—I think he just created it for tricks, to make them think it was a really good blow job or something, and then his face just naturally made itself up that way during any sex. For a while, though, I thought it was just for me, cuz what we had was so special and all that shit, and it was one of the things that made me fall for him. But anyway, even if his face was kinda unformed and hardwired and could perform only three looks successfully, Derek still tried to show a range of emotions. The look he gave me when he finally found his crystal was one of them—an awkward, apologetic ambivalence, composed by lifting his eyebrows up, pushing his chin down, and extending the right side of his mouth like he had some kinda slow tic. This was his "I did something that was a little fucked up" look, and he got away with murder with it, even though nobody believed he was truly regretful. Derek wasn't sorry about anything he did. That's just the way he was: if he slipped on the ice and tripped his grandma for her last fall, he'd offer up the same look and take the money out of her purse. But nobody cared. That was Derek. "Got some more fucking crystal," he'd say. "What a shitty drug. I got champagne tastes on a crystal budget though," which was really irritating cuz he said it all the time, cuz he probably didn't remember he said it all the time, even though I told him, and cuz he fucked up the meaning of the cliché—if you got champagne tastes on a crystal budget, you buy the champagne, but you run yourself into debt, don't you? I don't know. I never bothered to really figure it out. It just annoyed me.

But that's just cuz I hated Derek for getting away with everything, for being so goddamned self-centered that you couldn't hold anything against him; he would never think of you anyway, so why not just give in. So what if he said the same fucking thing almost every day and he was a crystal addict—we were in San Francisco, what else were we going to do? Besides, I liked that he got crystal, cuz whenever we were pissed off, we could just do a little and I would get an instant hard-on. Derek put his hand on my cock when I first snorted crystal to see how quickly the stuff went to my groin.

That's how he got me in the first place—picked me up at a vegetarian burrito place in the Mission and took me home one afternoon, threw me on the bed, took out his bag of speed, and held it out for me. We didn't leave for forty-eight hours. I swear. Two days in his little crappy Tenderloin studio where you could hear the drag queen's stomach upstairs struggle with bad shrimp or death throes—every thirty minutes we heard this explosion of diarrhea and then a toilet flush that shook the bed. We fucked—it was incredible—my body was a million Lite-Brites on at one time, etc. I was high on speed and sex and high on that pale bratty face in front of me that looked like he had just wiped a load of snot on the back of his sleeve, and high on all the mysterious Derek history around me—a picture of Derek on Polk Street, huddled next to a girl, that was taken for one of those trend stories on male hustlers; collages of Derek on a mountain top with angels and syringes hovering about him; matches everywhere, usually with a guy's name on the back of them, comics of grotesque, squat colorful figures fucking each other in the ribs and other exotic places; children's storybooks; teen boys and old ladies ripped from their resting places in magazine spreads and entwined together in languorous perversion; dirty T-shirts, etc. When he left to get more speed, I looked in his journal. Put one of his dirty white briefs next to my nose and took a whiff. Felt like the world had disappeared outside. Feared Derek would never come back. Convinced myself I should leave and get back to waiting for my unemployment check. Began jacking off. When Derek came back with more crystal, he got himself hard, started fucking me, rained a little crystal on my back, snorted it, then told me to switch and do the same. I couldn't get hard so I finger-fucked him and did the crystal from his back anyway. I moved into his place a week later.

Derek got me into hustling. I called it sex work because I went to college and lived in San Francisco, but he just called it hustling. He kept on telling me I'd be really good at it, that guys would like the tough-guy act I was putting on, that I could be a great top, that I could learn S/M and pull in thousands of dollars, that I thought I was better than him, that he was sick and tired of feeling like a slut, that if I hustled it would improve our relationship, etc. But my unemployment checks were still coming in, so I told Derek to fuck off; he got that don't-fuck-with-me look when we argued about this, so I knew nothing could stop him, and it was just a matter of time. A few weeks later Derek told me that his major trick, John (a john named John, ha ha), had spotted me walking next to Derek and really wanted to have me in bed. He said he'd pay three hundred dollars extra to have me and Derek in bed with him, so I did it. Derek and I did a little crystal, and we ended up at this megahouse in Twin Peaks with white carpeting everywhere, silver and glass tables, bookshelves, expensive coffee table editions of black-and-white male nude photo collections—the whole thing. John was allegedly a doctor who made a fortune selling drugs and prescriptions to users throughout California. Or at least that's what Derek told me. When John opened the door, I hadn't known what to expect, but it wasn't what I saw—an Izod and shorts over a surprisingly buoyant, round body. His hair was straight and thick and almost totally white, and he had that kinda gay face that somehow stays "boyish" until age one hundred or something. He was really friendly, but there was something cold in his eyes. John shook my hand and smiled at me like he had already fucked me a couple weeks ago and I'd loved it or something, like he knew something about me. John ushered us into the bedroom and asked us to get comfortable, got us drinks, and Derek started fooling around in bed. It was the same as when we fooled around at home after I got over the weirdness of it all, except every few minutes Derek would turn around and ask, "Is it okay?" or "Do you want us to do anything else?" or "Can you see everything?" John sat on his faux-fur-upholstered chair, his head propped up on his fist, totally impassive, like he was studying a particularly tough engineering problem. Derek and I were like arms and legs and an extra pair of eyes. When Derek yelled that he was getting close, John yelled out, "Don't come yet!" and got on his knees next to the bed. Derek pulled out of me and came all over John's face. Derek told me to do the same, so I did. John stroked us for a little afterward, his head resting on Derek's inner thigh; John was sitting on the carpet, rambling about getting another designer for his place. He wanted to make it more "California," with lots of redwood. Our come was glazing his face, and it dripped down slowly onto the rug. John went into the shower and Derek told me that we should leave, that John didn't wanna see us after he came out, so we walked out and grabbed six hundred dollars off the kitchen counter. Derek went back in—said he forgot something—then came out five minutes later.

It was my first trick, and I felt like—what—I had gotten over on someone, I guess, and thought Derek would like me more. I felt something—a heat, a high, a rush, but I never really savored the rush, cuz we hooked up with our dealer quick and abandoned the next week in a crystal ice storm. We fucked forever and spent the noncrystal money on Bikini Kill and Huggy Bear discs, matching nipple piercings, and a little silver Victorian coke spoon Derek had been eyeballing for months. I told Derek I loved him while he was fucking me one night, and then he took it as a mantra, spitting the words out in a whisper, over and over again, matching it with his thrusts until he shot in me. I asked him to keep his cock in me as we lapsed into sleep, and he did, but when I woke up, he was on the other side of his bed, and I was empty.

John paged again the next week and wanted both of us there. He told Derek he wanted us to play dress up—he had some kinda cutoff blue jeans fantasy, but we didn't have any, so we stopped off at one of the Mission thrift stores to pick up a couple pairs before we got there. John was a little pissed off that we didn't have the stupid cutoffs on, but his smile never flagged; it just got brittle, and his cold round eyes got a little slittier. Derek and I went into John's marble-and-mirror bathroom and changed into the cutoffs, and when we got into the bedroom, John was on his furry chair again, with no pants, slowly jacking off. He asked Derek if he had got the stuff, and Derek kinda grunted, extra surly, and fished in his pockets forever for the crystal. I didn't know about the deal—Derek musta been holding out on me, but he would have just told me that he forgot about it, so I pretended not to care. John grabbed his little hand mirror, like old Hollywood starlets have—gilded silver with lots of swirls on the back—and laid out a coke-size line. Derek told him that the stuff was strong, but John did the whole line, and then offered us some, which we did. John looked all crystalled out—like he was on the edge of some big discovery but couldn't quite get there. He told us to start making out, to take our shirts off, etc.—and then he told Derek to fuck me. I looked back while I was on my stomach to see John's eyes fixed on a spot in front of his face and his tongue rushing in and out of his mouth like one of those New Year's Eve noisemakers. When Derek and I shot, John snuck up right next to the bed and sprinkled his come on us. He went into the shower. Derek and I both dressed, and were gonna walk out, but John yelled for Derek to stay, so he did. "Dude, I gotta stay. I'll meet you at home," Derek said, with the shrug-smile he had nailed down.

I stopped in Castro Station for a beer cuz no one I knew would be at that shit-ass crystal-troll palace, then walked up Market, figuring Derek was gonna be there, but he wasn't. The crystal was still fucking with my mind, so I cleaned the whole damn place, twice, and even rearranged what furniture we had—which pretty much consisted of swapping the futon with the beanbag and moving the plants that Derek had bought when he decided he needed more nature in his life. Derek still hadn't come home, so I just stayed in, waiting for Derek to get back so we could hang.

Derek didn't come back for two days. I made three mix tapes, looked through my old journals, painted the ceiling of the bathroom silver, organized all of our CDs according to genre (punk, seventies, fucked-up experimental stuff, rap, etc.), and tried to write one poem for each of Derek's piercings—nose, eyebrow, guiche, bellybutton, nipple. Each time I finished a poem I was pissed off even more that Derek wasn't there, cuz I wanted him to come loping through the door while I was doing this stupid, romantic, literate thing for him. But he didn't come back until three or four a.m. a couple days later. I was drunk. I was pissed. We got into a fight. He said I wasn't his mother. He told me that John and he had spent a couple days fucking around, that he had bought him a couple hundred bucks worth of speed, that John was fucking crazy for him, that John couldn't get it up for the last day so he just spent the whole time jacking off his soft cock while Derek posed for him. Derek showed me the money in his pocket—seven hundred dollars—and said John wanted to take him on a trip to New York next week. I wanted to fuck around, but Derek was worn out—the last thing he wanted to do was deal with his cock. He spent a few hours in the corner drawing in his journal; one drawing was a skeleton fucking an ape. If you can imagine it, there was a lot of love in the drawing—the ape was kinda pouting—but that's where the warmth stopped. Derek wouldn't hug me or touch me or kiss me, and I jacked off in the futon, pissed that John had sucked all the play out of Derek.

Derek didn't sleep with me that night, or the next night, or the next night. I mean sleep in both ways—he didn't spoon me while we were dreaming, and he didn't fuck me in the ass. He was bingeing. I was pissed off at him, so I pretended not to want any crystal cuz it was getting on my nerves, but really I was doing crystal, just not with him. Derek didn't say much when he stopped home to change clothes or grab something to eat—just mumbled something about some trick up in Pacific Heights or hanging out with some bull dyke named Mikee—but I figured he had picked up a couple guys and fucked for days like he did with me that first time. Maybe it was the crystal—I had no evidence—just the acid inside me.

Then Derek's friend Jason overdosed. He was this kid Derek used to hang out with on Polk Street; he turned Derek on to speed, then moved on to smack. He died at his place down at Folsom and Twenty-fifth, just like that, he elapsed. Derek got the call when he was in the shower; he ran out naked, then just stood there with the phone hanging from his hand. We both went to Jason's apartment, just cuz Derek needed to do something, needed to see the body or the place Jason died, or whatever. We took a cab to the Mission, and I held Derek's hand, in between our legs, like we were trying to hide something from the world, or from each other. When we got there, the body was gone. Jason's roommates—John and Boa—were smoking cigarettes in the common room, talking about whether they could get into trouble with the cops, whether the landlord could evict them, etc. Derek wanted to leave—he hated those guys—and when we walked out, he told me that they had killed Jason, that Jason had quit smack a half a year ago, that Boa hated Jason cuz he had slept with John, etc. I thought Derek was crazy, that he just needed to unload, etc., but he kept on it and threatened to call the cops, wanted them put in jail. Then he got all silent. We walked all the way to the Tenderloin. Derek grabbed my hand, and I gave him my sweatshirt, cuz he was really cold. We sat outside our place on the steps, smoking cigarettes, and Derek got all serious, said he didn't want to die alone, said we should go up to Oregon and get out of the city, just live in a little cabin next to a river or something. When we got inside, we did some crystal, and we started messing around, but it wasn't sexual; it was to soothe each other. We just spread ourselves on each other like cream, and we kissed each other a lot. Derek looked into my eyes; his cold blue eyes had darkened a bit, and they seemed on the verge of tears. It was like an ecstasy trip or something—we felt each other's presences or auras ooze out of our bodies and share the bed with us. That night, Derek hung on to me harder than he ever had, closer than he ever had, burying his body in the twists of mine, and I caressed his arm, over and over again, like a piece of beautiful wood.

The next morning, Derek got up, lit some sage, and sat down and meditated. I had seen him do this before—the last time was the first week we were hanging out; he told me he had to clear his mind to see if we could live with each other—the answer was yes. This time he emerged out of a few minutes of Indian-style sitting and told me he wanted to quit hustling. He wanted to get a job, a real job, any job; he could do outreach for street kids—he'd already been offered the gig, he said. He told me I should quit too, that we should both go straight, that if we really loved each other we'd do that for each other. He had that possessed, bulldog look, scrunching up his nose and furrowing his brow, willing his idea into existence.

He'd take a week, he told me, to finish up with his clients and save up some money, but that was it, and we should both start looking for jobs. I hugged him, and I guess I got this image of both of us helping each other to imagine something different, something beautiful, having the courage to change, etc. Derek had a mind of switches and knobs, while mine was all analog dial—he could just toggle something in there, up or down, and everything would change, in a second, permanently.

The first thing he did was go and get more crystal. He said he needed it to get through the week, that this was the most important week in his life and he had to be up for it, etc. Then he called up a few of his regulars and told them that he was getting out of the business— me and my boyfriend, he kept on saying, we're gonna move to Oregon. I guess he'd changed his mind about getting a job in the city— that's how I learned most of the stuff about Derek's decisions; he would never tell me. I'd just learn it when he told somebody else, like it was something he had figured out a long time ago.

That week went like this: Derek got a book on Oregon, decided he wanted to live in Eugene, gave half of his clothes and CDs away to friends, had a few dates, showed me the pictures he kept in a little shoebox in the closet, put crystal on his cock and fucked me, and bought a pile of crystal to get us through the first few weeks in Oregon. We went partying with his friends almost every night, mostly whores Derek used to hang out with, dykes he trusted, a couple of artist types, etc. Derek was saying good-byes—one night he did ecstasy and everybody he ran into in the streets was suddenly his best friend; he held everybody's hands and turned eight years old, reciting slowly and precisely where they met and what memory he cherished of them, etc. It looked like he was really gonna do it, that we were really gonna do it—go to Oregon. That night, we stayed out all night, climbed up on top of this little cliff outside of the Castro, and looked at the little cookie-cutter domestic skyline that is San Francisco. It was way cold and windy—we had to smoke the pot.

We were at home watching *Pink Flamingos*—Derek loved John Waters, thought he was the most brilliant guy around—he had his own copy of the movie and knew all the lines. Whenever anybody wanted Derek to do anything political—like sign a petition or go to a medical marijuana protest or whatever—he'd turn them down and say, "Filth is my politics; filth is my life!" I thought it was cool and didn't figure out the reference 'til that night, when Divine makes her manifesto. Anyway, right after that, John paged. He wanted us to get over there. So we cabbed it, and we put those stupid cutoff blue jeans on in the cab, taking our pants off right in the back. Derek didn't wear any underwear—he dared me to suck his cock right there, and I did, cuz I'll do anything on a dare. When we got to John's place, he was waiting for us; he was real twitchy and couldn't stop moving his mouth around, crystal marks. I figured he'd been up for at least a day. John touched me and Derek all creepily, on the chest, moving down to the stomach, and then got all courtly, asking us if we wanted coffee, if the house was too cold or too warm, if we wanted to listen to different music (it was some stupid Steely Dan), if we wanted coffee, if we wanted crystal, whatever. So we did a couple bumps of crystal and then went to sit at the glass table in the kitchen, while John moved back and forth from the cabinet to the countertop, making coffee. He was talking all the time—his medical office was being run by idiots; the nurses were all gossips, except for this one guy who was really cute and maybe raiding the stash of local anesthetics; he met this really sexy guy and did we know him; coffee is really his drug of choice, etc. Derek would say something back to John, and roll his eyes to me like, "When do we get the fucking money?"

It seemed like an hour, but we were doing bumps of crystal, so in a very long five minutes, the coffee was done. By that time John didn't want it anymore and neither did we, so we just went into the bedroom and John told us to take our shirts off but leave the cutoffs on. He told us to start, to go on, and so we did. Derek's mouth tasted like it always tasted—tobacco and that bitter pharmaceutical crystal tinge—and we passed our chewing gum to each other during the kiss like a secret message. John jacked off his crystal-crippled cock and kept on saying, "Yeah, that's it," like bad porn. Derek pushed me on the bed and moved me on my stomach, like we usually do it. He started getting the lube out and smearing it in my ass crack, when John said, "Why do you always fuck him? Next time you're gonna get fucked." Derek kept on going but said, "There isn't gonna be a next time." John asked, "What does that mean?" Derek told him, "We're moving to Oregon!" John got up and stood right next to the bed, his soft cock peeking out from below the bottom of his shirt. "What do you mean you're moving to Oregon?" he asked. Derek pulled off of me and told him he was sick of this town and he was leaving. "When?" John asked. "Two days," Derek said, "going to Portland." I reached for a cigarette.

John told Derek that he didn't want him to go, that he needed someone to go to New York with him, and that Derek had already agreed to go. Derek said, "Yeah, well you never brought it up again." John said, "Well, I'm going, next week." I figured John was lying cuz why would he suddenly mention that he was leaving in four days and that he expected Derek to go with him? It was total bullshit. John said, "So, are you gonna come with me?" Derek said, "I can't, dude. I'm moving to Oregon." John sat back down in his faux-fur-covered chair, to get more leverage or something. He stared at Derek like Derek stood between him and five million dollars, like an obstacle to be surmounted.

"You can move after we come back."

Derek didn't know what to say to that; he squirmed a little and looked at me for help, so I said, "We've got everything planned," which we didn't. I didn't even know that Derek wanted to move to Portland until now. John was pissed. I'd never seen him like this—he pulled some strange authority out of his ass, like he was back in the doctor's office giving someone a prescription. "You've never been to New York, have you? But you want to go." Derek didn't know where to go now. He changed positions on the bed, sitting up against the headboard. "Yeah, dude, of course," he said. "So come and see it." "I don't know dude." "I'm paying your airfare; we're staying in a great hotel . . ." Derek asked, "And?" John said, "And I'm giving you a hundred dollars a day spending money."

Derek motioned for my cigarette, so I gave it to him, and he pulled a drag. I still remember looking up at him while his lips were forming around the filter, waiting for his answer. Derek didn't look at me. He just looked straight at John and said, "Okay." John said, "Great," and then started working his cock again. "You guys should go back to work."

So I turned over on my stomach and Derek started fucking me again. I played dead. I left when John went into the shower, said, "See you at home, dude." Derek ran after me, playing dumb. "What?" he asked. "Is it about the New York thing? I've always wanted to go to New York. We can go to Oregon after I get back." But after that, he didn't say another word about Oregon. It was all New York—I'm going to New York, he told everyone he was going to New York; he started playing the Velvet Underground over and over again, etc. Every time I talked to him about Oregon his eyes glazed over and he changed the subject. John picked up Derek in a taxi at our place a few mornings later. Derek kissed me good-bye and told me he'd call, left, then came back and grabbed his baseball cap, then left again.

Derek did leave a message, from the top of the Empire State Building. He claimed to be calling from John's cell phone and said he could see all the way to our place and that I should close the window. When he got back into town, he looked like hell. Told me he hadn't slept in four days, that John and he had done all the crystal that was supposed to keep us in Oregon for a month, that he was sorry, but John had asked him to move in and was willing to pay him lots-o-cash just to live there, so he was gonna live there. I wanted to talk about it, but Derek told me John was waiting outside with the taxi, and he had to run—just wanted to pick up some more clothes. I said, "Wait! We gotta talk about this! What's going on? Are you living there forever? Are you giving up the apartment? What should I do?" He was running around, looking for something, and he said, "We'll deal with it." I turned into the spurned lover. I said, "I thought you wanted to get out of the business. I thought you wanted to live with me in Oregon." Derek was on his way out, but he turned before he reached the door and said what he always says: "Dude, I've got champagne tastes on a crystal budget. It's time for some champagne."

Getting Fucked

Christopher Boyd

"Welcome home, Christopher."

Each weekend as I entered the Apollo Room, the dim sitting area off the Gaiety stage, where deals were struck and smoking was allowed, I heard this warmly predictable greeting from the Gaiety's self-appointed ringmaster and scorekeeper, Bill, a foul-smelling little man in a musty sweater and thick, hazy glasses. He knew, or professed to know, everything about everyone, as it related to the Gaiety, and he kept copious notes to prove it.

"Thanks, Daddy." The call and response was always the same when I reported for duty on Friday afternoon, but the evenings were always different, like the pages of a sordid book you can't read fast enough. Would I finish the night with five hundred dollars in the pocket of my torn-at-the-ass Levi's, or spend my last dollar on the Number Six train home and walk the thirty blocks back tomorrow to try my luck again? That uncertainty was one of my favorite things about hustling, and one of the truest pleasures of living in New York.

For three years, I hustled out of the Gaiety Burlesque Theatre in Times Square, the relic above Howard Johnson's on Forty-sixth Street. The Gaiety is an old-school porno theater with class, salacious and civilized, a thinking man's bordello, where Gypsy Rose Lee is rumored to have peeled a glove and popped a balloon. Pay your ten dollars to one of the silent Greek sisters at the front window—the word was they owned the place, but they weren't talking—and you can sit in one of the darkened rows of red velveteen seats watching some random porn on the wide-screen video projector. But when the music begins, gentlemen, please feel free to move closer to the stage to get a look at all of those handsome Gaiety dancers.

The makeshift video screen gets tucked away, and red and blue lights spread across the stage. The shiny black runway licks the audience as silver metallic fringe surrounds the action from floor to ceiling like an amateur talent contest. But there are no amateurs on this stage. Muscle boys and skinny boys, black, white, Canadian boys and college boys—all dance, one by one, removing their tight white T-shirts and unzipping to flash a shock of white briefs. Soapy fresh, short-haired, and clean shaven, the Gaiety boy is your fantasy college roommate, the medal-winning diver, strutting around the room before he showers. As the lights dim—not yet!—the half-naked pony trots offstage, and you are forced to sit in the dark, the pounding drums anticipating his return. Finally, he eases onstage, with a bobbing sing-a-long erection, and shows you in delicious full-color detail what you, yes you, can rent between shows. See anything you like?

I would walk the Gaiety runway for a full week (seven days, six shows a day; that's forty-two onstage erections a week, with hope-fully as many offstage) before each semester to pay my film school tuition, and then I would work occasional weekends to cover rent and food. At $150 a pop I could make $600 to $1,000 a weekend. Add to that regular clients calling for a midweek rendezvous, and I had a living. A living, yes, but not a film.

See, I was hustling to put myself through documentary film classes at NYU, and I needed something to show for those years, a student film to tempt producers and agents into making me their next Big Thing. Well, I had recently met a death-defying diva from the fifties, a woman who had been through Broadway, film, cabaret, television, drugs, motherhood, unemployment, men, and disco. She was a legend, a role model whose records I would lip-synch long before I knew how to masturbate. I not only met this diva, but got her to agree to participate in a film about her life—directed by me, a film school sophomore. I was in way over my head, but here was my *Citizen Kane*, my *Mean Streets*, a project to jettison my star into the cinematic solar system, and beyond. My film would reignite her lagging career, but she would die, tragically, on the cusp of her comeback, fueling a huge postmortem resurgence in Everything Diva. As the world's greatest scholar on the Diva's life and work, I would be asked to curate film festivals and photography collections. I would publish the authorized biography, *The Last Days*, and retire in the south of France, where I would establish a foundation in her name for orphaned teenage boys. But first, I needed to make a film. And to make a film, I needed money. And, by now, I knew where to look. Thank God I learned how to masturbate.

I found out in May that my diva was to be a featured performer at the Edinburgh Theatre Festival that August in Scotland. Here was my opportunity to make my film an international product, expand my European market, and add a shitload of class. I had to go. And I had to have a camera and a plane ticket—there was a lot of fucking that needed to take place before August. (Actually, in all honesty, no real on-the-job anal intercourse ever took place. Besides the viral risk, I wanted to save something sexual for my private life, a part of me that couldn't be bought. And no client ever asked me to fuck them because, I assume, the look I worked was cute, young bottom boy, and all of the clients who were looking to get fucked would hire a straight-acting horse-hung football or boxing type to pound their old queer ass. Whatever.) I had less than three months to charm the masses of men who would fund my art. The prospect was daunting, overwhelming, exhausting to consider. I pictured the necessary fifty or sixty men lined up outside a hotel room, twisting hungrily around the hallway, down the stairs, and out onto the street. But capitalism thrives in one of two ways: high volume or high quality. I could sell sixty hamburgers or one steak au poivre. Well, what would you do?

"Only two other gay boys here tonight, Christopher," Ringmaster Bill announced. How he came up with his figures, and how the other eleven dancers who fucked old men for a living could convince themselves or anyone else they were straight, is unanswerable. But Bill was usually right. He knew who had slept with whom, what they did, and how much it cost. As long as I knew him, he never took anyone home. Perhaps, if he had enough information, a long enough list of sordid details to form a complete fantasy, he never actually had to go through with it. I imagine he was the happiest man there.

Bill could be useful. He introduced me that evening to New Jersey John, using an at-last-they-meet tone typically reserved for comic strip superheroes meeting their cartoon nemeses. "Mr. Beck, this is Christopher, a Texan and star student at NYU. He's older than he looks. Christopher, meet John Beck, a prominent New Jersey lawyer and an admirer of all things preteen." What I saw before me was a seventeenth-century duke, a man roughly two-thirds the size of Rhode Island. Tall, girthy, and robust, John was a red-cheeked Falstaff with a bushy strawberry-blond wig. His sweaty, jowly face betrayed a great appetite for food, for sex, for life—in that order. His tiny eyes, at turns jolly then beady, were obscured by roaming eyebrows crawling up his forehead like kudzu. He grinned the grin of a crocodile, the grin they must teach in law school, as he twisted a smile from his greasy, lipless mouth. A heart attack in penny loafers, John was keenly intelligent and watchful, every word chosen and each move made with chesslike precision and pomp.

We sat talking in the Apollo Room for hours that night, drinking the vodka-spiked orange punch and licking the salt off pretzel sticks. In my nine months at the Gaiety, I had developed a lure that worked well on small and medium fish. Would it work on the Great White John? At first, I treated him with my usual thrust and parry of aloofness and intimacy. Deflect a personal question, stroke his cheek; push him away, draw him in. Keep him off balance, find his need, then figure out how to fill it. Almost fill it. Fill it just enough to make his desire unbearable. Everyone has one basic need, a single deep yearning, whether or not they are even aware of it. But if you watch and listen, they will always reveal it to you. John wanted to flirt; he needed to know I was interested and interesting, so I returned his verbal volleys with triple entendres as we spoke of his law practice, my youth in Texas, his favorite restaurants, my favorite hotels. We talked about South Beach and Paris. He said he preferred Fort Lauderdale, and I suggested London.

"I'm going back in August," he offered. He's rich, he likes me, and he's going to Europe in August. I gave a silent thanks to the patron saint of hustlers.

"August? Really? So am I. We should meet for tea."

"How about a late supper. Tonight."

Meals are a delicate proposition between hustler and client. If you agree to a $20 meal, you might lose a $200 client. But dinner is an investment. You have to be willing to sacrifice a pawn to capture a queen. A john knows, and this John did, that a hustler agreeing to dinner is a coup, a compliment. As a hustler, your time is money, and he just got something for nothing. He likes that. But letting a john get to know the real you crosses a dangerous line—solid fantasies are not built on the shallow sands of reality.

"I would enjoy that."

His eyes were aglow with flirtation, the sparkle of an amorous hippo, as he watched my next show, which I performed for John and John only, locking eyes with him as I teased off my snug black Calvin boxers to swing my stiff dick and bent over to present my meaty white ass. The lonely, desperate voyeurs in the audience turned to spot the object of my affection. John nodded like a proud papa, licking his mouth where his lips should be.

Four months would pass before I would find John's extensive collection of Eastern European child pornography, sexless boys from Krakow rubbing their hairless pubes like fifth-grade girls. Six months would pass before he would show me his dungeon in the damp basement of his parents' New Jersey home. His deceased parents. The basement was dark and moist, smelling of fertilizer and oil, with farm implements hung from the low ceiling like rusty artifacts in a de Sade museum. A small platform, a stage really, was outfitted with leather ankle restraints chained to either side, forcing the victim to stand spread-eagled. Wrist restraints were bolted to the beam above. On a nearby shelf, next to watering cans and nails, was a full selection of classic torture equipment, rubber ball gags and leather whips, chrome leg spreaders and anal probes. An entire year would pass before I would agree to be restrained. But I'm getting ahead of myself—I had yet to find out about any of this.

I met John for dinner that first night, and for a month, we repeated a dance, a game, a seduction—although at the time I wasn't sure who was doing the seducing. Night after night, we shared drinks, dinners, and long talks over bottles of California sparkling wine. I clutched his porcine hand, his thick golden pinky ring snug against my palm, as we walked up Fifth Avenue from his favorite restaurant on West Twelfth Street, through Union Square Park, to my room at Hotel 17. Dressed in our charcoal or black suits with jewel-tone ties and starched collars, John would press me against the iron grating outside my hotel, as we shared a smooch and traded compliments between giggles and coos: Thanks for dinner, Thank you for joining me, It was my pleasure, No it was mine. Finally, Jimmy, the rockabilly hotel manager with a scraggly goatee, would stick his head out the front office window. "You two need a room?"

I waved him away with a laugh and a roll of the eyes. "I should go."

"Good night, sweet prince, a flock of angels fly thee to thy rest."

There is no appropriate response to paraphrased Shakespeare. I said nothing. Instead, I managed a look that was a combination of flattered, awed, and turned on. My first college major was acting; I never dreamed it would be so useful. John watched me climb the stoop, and I took one last glance back ("I want to remember this night forever"), as I entered the door.

"Hey, whore," was Jimmy's welcome home. He liked the idea of having a prostitute living in the hotel, along with the drag queens and models and musicians, upholding the hotel's Weimar sheen.

"Could you wait a little longer next time?" I sneered, "He didn't have time to get my underwear off."

I could hear Jimmy laughing as the elevator door swung shut.

John and I repeated this scene week after week, romantic and sexless. And after a long chaste month, John finally proposed over dinner.

"Have you made plans yet for your trip to London?"

Bingo. Touchdown. He fucking swallowed it; now reel him in, nice and easy. I inhaled slowly, regulating my heartbeat, and looked up from my tiramisu calmly, disinterested, eyelids at half-mast. "I haven't had a chance. I should go ahead and do that."

"Well, I'm taking a fifteen-day trip to London, Paris, Amsterdam, and Munich, and I would like you to go with me."

"With you? I'll have to check the dates. I mean, I'm very flattered. But you know it's a working trip for me, what with the film—"

"We'll make arrangements for the film."

I paused, flushed, and looked up to meet his eyes. What I finally said was a breathy, "Thank you." But I was thinking: How do I make it through two more idling months of handholding and with-holding? Is it too late to opt for the sixty men in the hallway?

I wanted to coast to August, but would he go for it? Could I avoid sexual contact for two more months? If we have sex, do I charge him for it? What if he doesn't like it? Would he cancel the trip? Get another whore? And how do I manage the fifteen-day trip? Does he own me for the two weeks we're away? Was it going to be nonstop sex in Europe? After our arrival, I would go to Edinburgh to shoot for three days. Could I go home after Edinburgh? Could I afford to? Would he let me? Would I have to tell him?

Of course, I agreed to go. I was thrilled and relieved to have made my goal, but I couldn't enjoy it. The approach I took over the next two months sounded like a cheap nail polish: vaguely amo-rous. And it worked. If you don't make any promises, you can never break them. I continued the romantic shtick and played chaste ("I'm not ready to have sex") and let his imagination fill in the rest. Not until we got to London did I discover what a fertile imagination was cooking under that wig.

We arrived in London on Tuesday morning and went straight to Claridge's, an English cliché of crystal, marble, and disdainful doormen—a concoction swallowed only by the queen and Ameri-can tourists. Our suite was outfitted with upholstered walls in striped lavender and heather brocatelle, and dozens of bells to ring for some sort of service: a bell by the phone, a bell by the toilet, a bell by the doorbell, and, over the bathtub, a green silk cord with a golden tassel hanging low enough to tug without lifting your white ass from the warm milk bath. The room was accented with china ashtrays and original oil paintings, leather-bound literature and fresh flowers. The white-on-white tiled bathroom was filled with bathing sheets, towels, towelettes, and washcloths, all white and warm and monogrammed with a royal blue C. More flowers. I spent one full hour walking numbly around the room, opening cupboards and touching walls, turning on faucets and adjusting the settings of the myriad chandeliers, table lamps, and sconces. Does anyone really live like this? How did I ever live without it? If my friends could see me now.

After unpacking, we spent a leisurely day doing the London food tour—stopping in Regent's Park for tea and scones and in Piccadilly

Circus for a pint of warm lager and kidney pie—John's idea of cultural exchange. After an afternoon rest at the hotel, a bubble bath and shave, we had the first of many three-hour feedings. Tonight was The Connaught, a hotel and restaurant so exclusive you had to request a reservation by mail. After several dirty vodka martinis and beluga with blinis, we were swept into a simple and elegant dining room, dark wood wainscoting with cream walls and tablecloths. A silver candlestick reigned in the middle of the table, next to a white ceramic vase of lilies and freesia. Our dinner began with asparagus cream soup and a seeded flatbread; a smooth and sweet she-crab salad soon followed, accompanied by a mélange of grilled miniature vegetables. A Blenheim bottled water was joined by a bottle of crisp Roederer champagne. John seemed surprised that I found my way through the maze of flatware and pleased that we could agree the champagne was bold but amusing. My main course was a grilled lamb lounging in a rich rosemary reduction, joined by sides of a parmesan creamed spinach and potatoes soufflé, thinly sliced and puffed into delicate hollow balls. We found the bottle of meaty Bordeaux brashly sophisticated. Then came a perfectly creamy and crusty crème brûlée, scorched an oaky brown and served with a light dessert white. A silver platter of bite-sized tarts of fruit and noisettes, chocolate and custard, arrived next, soon followed by black coffee and bittersweet chocolate truffles. And a twenty-year-old cognac— why splurge on our first night?

The conversation was full and easy, filled with pauses, as we closed our eyes and relished the hundreds of dollars and thousands of calories we were eating like pigs to slop. We laughed at the day's events and engaged the waiter or the wine steward or the maître d' in a chat about the city or nightlife, the restaurant's history or the menu, predictably followed by a half-hour debate on the nature of the server's sexuality. Gay or straight? Top or bottom? Romantic or nasty?

By the time we walked past the doormen at Claridge's, my body was shutting down from the glut of sauces and meats and sugars and liquors. We climbed the white marble staircase to our second-floor suite and collapsed in the living room, our jackets tossed over the leather wing-back chairs, pants unbuttoned, ties askew. Our eyes met, and I returned his grin with a smile. Mine was in appreciation for what had passed. His was in anticipation of what was to come.

"Are you ready for bed?" was what he asked. What I heard was, "Do you have any idea how much today cost? Between the flight, the cabs, the meals, the hotel, the tips? Not to mention the tab for the last three months. Are you ready to pay back Poppa?"

"Sure," I answered (which you will please note is not a yes).

I took my clothes off deliberately, coquettishly, forgetting that he had already seen me butt naked some half-dozen times over the course of the summer, wagging my hard-on and shaking my cheeks for a crowd of two hundred. The pants were folded on the pants hanger, the tie and belt rolled carefully and placed in the bureau. Maybe he would pass out before I finished. The starchy shirt was rehung for another night. I could not, would not, watch him undress. Padding into the bathroom in my plaid boxers, I brushed my teeth, and by the time I returned, John was in bed. His enormous body was draped in green and gold brocade, as if a pair of curtains had attacked and swallowed him whole, his wig still attached. Would he wear it all night? Should I tell him I know? Does he know I know? I slowly walked around to my side and crawled under, leaving my boxer shorts on. We were both exhausted from the day and overstuffed from the evening, but I knew it was my responsibility to initiate something sexual. It was the right thing to do, the only thing to do, but I feinted and went for the cuddle-and-pass-out. He rolled away from me for a moment, dragging the covers with him, and turned off his bedside sconce. Lights out, good sign. Very good sign. Most johns wanted to see what they were paying for.

I draped myself over his supine body, nesting my head into mounds of chest hair, against his silver-dollar nipples. He smelled like a musty baby, talcum powder, sweet perfume, and stale body odor combining to form a scent that, although not unpleasant, brought out the wrong images: visions of diapers and mom and pink round flesh. I nuzzled him, making a couple of cooing sounds, a petite Fay Wray to his King Kong. Please fall asleep. Either of us. Both of us. Now. I began to breathe slowly and deeply, both lulling myself into slumber and attempting to convince him I was already asleep. He took my head in his hands and tilted it up to meet his mouth and tongue. John was not an outright bad kisser, but he had no lips, so it was either dry and asexual or all tongue and teeth. He kissed me like he was sucking a mango seed, slurping and chewing in large gulps. Then he rolled me off his chest and over onto my back. Here we go.

What was about to happen must have been a dirty super-eight loop that John had played over and over in his head, editing, replaying, perfecting, replaying. If he masturbated, he must have come to this scene a hundred times over the summer. He seduced me, wined and dined me, treated me like his sweet prince, with respect and adoration, affection and delicacy. I was a little seed he planted, watered, covered in dung, and watched grow. And now, at last, I was about to flower.

John sat up on his knees, naked, the duvet and sheet now crumpled to the floor around us. Reaching across to his side table drawer, he pulled out a travel-size yellow plastic squeeze bottle of Vaseline Intensive Care lotion, a prop he had clearly planted hours before, in anticipation. He squirted a greasy mound into his right hand, dropped the bottle on the bed, and grabbed both of my ankles with his left hand. He pulled my legs up toward the ceiling, like a baby about to be changed, a yearling about to be skinned, and smeared my ass with the lotion, saving a little to rub on his stiff little Pez-dispenser dick. He moved toward me, lifting my legs a little higher, and started to enter me.

"Wait." There were so many things wrong with this picture, I didn't know where to begin.

"What?" He was jolted out of his fantasy like a bear out of hibernation.

"Um—I don't get fucked."

"Excuse me?" This bear was not happy.

"And how could you even think of not using a condom?" I went on the offensive.

"I never use condoms." His voice was low and inexpressive, disbelief oozing down his cheeks and dripping off his chin like honey.

He rolled off me onto his back, and we both lay still for a tense minute. "We can do other things," I offered warmly, trying to regain the atmosphere of sex. Eager to show my eagerness, I grabbed his soft dick and started pulling at it, squeezing his balls. It shrank even further, lifeless and disappointed.

"I want you to fuck me." The request came from nowhere. I looked around to see who else must have come into the room, a randy bellman or errant maid. No client had ever asked me to penetrate them. And John had been so clearly intent on fucking me, I couldn't believe this request, rising like smoke from the rubble of this evening.

"If you want me to," I managed, not wanting to sound too eager and, well, not feeling too eager. John rolled onto his stomach, and I pulled a condom and lube out of my backpack. My cock is always hard. If I'm naked, I'm hard. (I'm sure this trait has its drawbacks, but I haven't found one yet, particularly in this business.) I rolled the condom down and crawled up to straddle John's thighs. The ass before me was a pasty plateau of flesh: pink, hairy, soft, and flat. I applied some lube onto the crack of his ass, in the general vicinity of his asshole, not wanting to stick my fingers into that crevasse. "Go slow. I've only been fucked once before." I lay on top of him like a jockey astride his horse and made a motion to insert my cock. The mound of flesh beneath me shuddered and I stopped. I tried again and made it completely inside this time.

Let me pause from this image to tell you that I love anal sex. I love getting heavy fucked by a beautiful stranger or held and made love to by the man of my dreams. And I will never forget the first time I fucked someone, a good two years after I started having sex. What an all-consuming feeling of passion and power, to have a man beneath me, submitting, releasing himself as the ecstasy cojoins and envelops us completely. This was not such an experience. There were no writhing bodies, no orgiastic moans or heated bites and kisses. No fingers and toes grabbing and curling in the overwhelming pleasure of pleasure. In the silence of our suite, all I could hear was the squish-squish of my dick as it dunked repeatedly into John's soggy asshole. I could feel nothing. There was no pleasure, no pain. I thought I could get off in any circumstance, a little pressure on my cock and off I go. No. All I could visualize was the tail end of John's intestines, rashed and shitty, wrapped around my sheathed dick as he lay lifelessly beneath me. I barely had a hard-on, and there was no way I was going to come. Since he couldn't pleasure himself by fucking me, a fantasy concocted over months, he was going to allow me the pleasure, the honor even, of fucking him. And I couldn't even manage to do that.

I rolled off him onto the bed, apologizing, running my fingers through the hair on his back. "I'm sorry. I'm just so tired; my body doesn't know what's happening. Between the travel and the food and the alcohol, I'm shot." John was looking in my direction, his eyes open, but he saw and heard nothing. I considered leaving, that night, right then. This whole trip was a mistake, a lie. I could feel the hatred, the regret, rising from his body like steam off asphalt. The disappointment. The realization that he had been hustled (but I never promised anything!). I curled up next to him as I had when we first crawled into bed a half hour before, only more slowly and carefully, waiting for him to push me away or hit me or do something or say anything. Nothing. I tried to clear my head, but the next two weeks kept encircling my thoughts like a ring of taunting children, teasing and mocking in endless sing-song rhyme.

–7–

Porn Moguls

Alvin Eros

On my first porn shoot, Lon Flexxx told me that if I wanted to get more video work, I ought to have a model's rep. Lon played a wandering bon vivant in a tuxedo whom I, improbably cast as a straight butch type, lured into my apartment for hot sex. The review in a local gay rag said that one of the highlights of the video was "scary Caligula look-alike Alvin Eros," and despite the unflattering association with one of Rome's most egregiously evil emperors, I felt it was a good review. I mean, they said highlights, not low points, right? Never having seen the video, I was astonished to read that my (admittedly somewhat nelly) voice had been dubbed over by someone who, according to the reviewer, sounded just like George Peppard. I wasn't too upset, since I've always loved him in *Breakfast at Tiffany's*. And anyway, I was given lines such as "I've killed for less!" to be delivered when Mr. Flexxx began fellating me. Could you make that sound convincing?

About a year later, I looked up a model's rep in LA. With no little trepidation (you never know when you'll be drugged, kidnapped, and sold into white slavery, do you?), I rang the bell of his charming little cottage, nestled on a leafy side street of some Hollywood hill. The rep, let's call him Brett, answered the door in white tennis shorts and a white polo top, his broad smile revealing truly enormous white teeth, his head sporting a stiff helmet of honey-blond hair. This was in the 1980s, and I couldn't help envisioning him as an extra milling around a tennis court on *Dynasty*. "Pleased to meet you," he said formally, with a manly handshake, after which he took me into his small office. He'd asked me to bring photos of myself, so I handed him some snapshots showing me nude in a variety of come-hither poses, while leaning against a gold Roman pedestal in front of a draped, blood-red curtain. The set does seem a little overwrought now that I think of it—perhaps the Caligula comparison went to my head.

After examining the photos, Brett spoke in a halting, embarrassed sort of way. "Frankly . . . they look a bit . . . artsy." He explained that he needed men who were "proud and masculine." He decided, however, to give me a chance, on two conditions. First, I had to cut my hair, which was dyed Clairol blue-black and super short, except for a wild mop of curls on top (totally New Wave), and, second, I'd need to lose some weight. Though I'd just been tactfully called a fat femme, I ignored my plummeting self-esteem and promised to drop a few pounds and visit a barber. I was pretty lucky to get any sort of a break, since guy-next-door types like me were fast being replaced by the steroid-built *Übermenschen* who dominate today's big-budget smut. As it happened, Brett was on his way to meet a producer, and I was invited to come along.

After a short ride in Brett's very new, very clean car, we arrived at an unprepossessing house and were greeted at the door by an unremarkable man, whom I'll call Mr. Producer. Stepping into the foyer, I was dismayed to behold the most appallingly tasteless living room I'd ever seen. Spotless and furnished in pseudocolonial Ethan Allen furniture, evoking a folksy, all-American style, it was somehow suffused (perhaps it was the surveillance cameras in the corners?) by a phony, setlike quality, making it seem nightmarishly authoritarian. Over the mantelpiece, on which sat photos of bland white people at graduations and weddings, was a stuffed deer's head. Behind the glass windows of a cupboard sat a series of astoundingly ugly, decorative, "special occasion" china. The bookshelves held finely bound classics of great literature, which one couldn't remove because in front of them were dozens of small, collectable pewter cowboys and Indians arranged as if in battle. One would have no trouble, in a room like that, believing that, in just a moment, Nancy Reagan would sweep in with a tray of big, gooey chocolate chip cookies and that crazy look in her eyes.

I hid my aesthetic revulsion by playing with a yipping purebred terrier that ran up to greet us. Bonding with the dog, I hoped, would make me look wholesome, uncomplicated, and therefore—in the perverted world of the gay sex industry—attractive. After introductions, we sat at a low coffee table and Brett began showing Mr. Producer a loose-leaf binder containing dirty photos of the models he'd signed.

After a few minutes, I heard a woman's voice singing softly in Spanish. As if on cue, Brett's and Mr. Producer's voices lowered and guilty, conspiratorial looks crept onto their faces. Suddenly, they scurried into the kitchen, taking the book with them, as a small Hispanic woman in an apron came into the room and began dusting some ceramic ducks. I followed the smut peddlers, who'd resumed their work next to the sink, discussing who'd look good sodomizing whom and so on. No sooner had they gotten back to work when they scuttled, roachlike, into an adjoining laundry room, setting the book on the dryer. Again I followed, and Brett, seeing the questioning look on my face, pointed to the woman, now coming into the kitchen to get some Lemon Pledge from under the sink. Smiling and waving, she bid hello to the pornographers, who in turn waved back. "Hi Esmerelda!" As she left, Brett silently mouthed the words, "We're not out to the maid."

Much to my surprise, I got a phone call a few months after the visit, inviting me to appear in a video in two weeks' time. Doing my best to look proud and masculine enough to deserve my five hundred dollars (half of what several other models were getting paid, I later learned inadvertently), I dieted, got a flattop, and borrowed some butch-looking clothes—Levi's and a plaid flannel shirt—from my roommate. Directors assign sexual partners with an eye only to their own lurid gratification, and I was ordered to get nasty with a variety of men to whom I wasn't particularly attracted. They were all quite proud and masculine, while I've always liked my men humble and androgynous. If you want to know what making porn is like, just pick up three or four guys you've never met before off the street, take them home, and set up an orgy under blazing hot lights, with several strangers standing around barking directions and the ground rules that everybody has to keep at least one orifice filled at all times while all facing in the same direction. Oh, and nobody can say anything intelligent or funny.

While on the shoot, I got a crush on the still photographer, a quiet, wispy little boy with a shock of sandy-blond hair falling over one eye: sort of Veronica Lake meets A Flock of Seagulls. I could imagine him writing hopelessly romantic letters to men who'd broken his heart and going for long walks on the beach at twilight. My crush evaporated when, to my everlasting shame, he made me pose in a backward baseball hat with a sleeveless T-shirt emblazoned with a silhouette of the Marlboro cowboy—I who so deeply abhors smoking, advertising, and cowboys! Fortunately, they didn't use the stills. I hope you won't think me too self-congratulatory, but I like to think it was because my essential nelly, artsy character shined through the facade of hypermasculinity, making the pictures insufficiently proud and masculine.

8

A Slice of "The Life"

Eileen Geoghegan

San Rafael, December 1978

The crisp night air pumped us up even higher. Lauren stuck Dylan's *Live at Budokan* tape in the deck as I guided the car onto the freeway. Tunes cranking, we flew through San Anselmo, Corte Madeira, and past Marin City. We took the Highway 1 exit and followed it to the legendary Mill Valley 7-Eleven. More money passed hands in that parking lot than at the Bank of America. Colleen was parked by the phone booth. I pulled up next to her. Drew's Porsche pulled up. He motioned for us to follow him up the little road next to the store.

As our parade climbed higher and higher up the mountain, the sleepy houses got fancier and farther apart. At the top, the road ended in a circular driveway. An Audi and Charlie's antique Mercedes roadster were already there. We parked in the circle behind them. Everyone got out. Four doors slammed shut. Drew came toward us and winked in the starlight.

"This is the big guy's place," he whispered, even though there was not another soul in the night. We knew he was wired. He gave each of us a kiss and said, "Anything goes. Don't worry about anything. We'll take good care of you."

Drew is a sweetheart, I thought, as we followed his bulky shadow, single file, down a flagstone path through several openings in a tall hedge. The place was swaddled in trees as though it were hiding. A faint clandestine glow seeped out of the side windows. There was a stained glass porthole in the door.

We entered the kitchen, which seemed like a redwood cave. A couple of giant candles on a big, round, oak table provided the only light. The candles were surrounded by bottles of Louis Jardot Pouilly Fusse, little plates with mounds of white powder, and ashtrays full of roaches. The air was thick with marijuana smoke and whispering.

"Fuckers are talking to themselves already," Lauren said under her breath. Drew introduced us to Craig, who made a grand gesture with his arm toward the table. "Help yourselves, girls," he said, and he passed us each a wine glass. Lauren sat down next to Charlie, who greeted her with, "Here come the coke hounds." They started arguing immediately. Colleen commandeered Drew into a tour of the house; they disappeared down a stairway hewn from tree trunks. A Navajo rug ran down the center. Craig filled my wine glass, took my arm, and led me down the brightly colored passage.

The living room was white adobe supported by dark wooden beams—très Santa Fe. There were paintings of Indians on the wall. I had seen lots of Curtis in the inner sanctums of the haute coke crowd. Craig invited me to stand next to the great, crackling fire. Redwood burl furniture with sheepskin seats encircled the stone hearth. Craig picked a mirror off the arm of one of the chairs and cut me a line.

"You're beautiful," he said, as I horned a line. "I want to tell you about my wife." He stared off, and I took a quaalude out of a little silver bowl on the mantle.

"That's a gorgeous lamp," I said, pointing to an orange tulip-shaped glass shade with an engraved lead base. I swallowed the lude with a swig of wine.

"That's nothing," said Craig. He grabbed my arm again, too tight this time, leading me to the far end of the room and up a discreet staircase. His bedroom was done up in New England antiques, a big four-poster in the center. It reminded me of home, Massachusetts. I was uncomfortable. I wanted to go back downstairs to New Mexico.

Craig motioned me to sit on a chair, then sat on the bed facing me. He picked up a plate of powder from the night table and started cutting more lines. I wished I'd grabbed a bottle of Jardot. This could be a while, I thought, as we each did a line.

"What do you want?" He asked.

Five hundred dollars and a gram," I replied, realizing I should've asked for twice as much. He took a bunch of crisp bills from an envelope in the drawer of the night table and handed them to me. Then he took another bill and scooped out a pile of coke from a baggy that was also in the drawer. Craig folded the coke up into the bill and gave it to me. Then he started talking.

"My wife broke my heart." He launched into his tale with such intensity that I didn't dare look away from him. I fumbled to stash the money in my pocket and wedged the coke down my boot, hoping it wouldn't melt. I realized that I was going to keep my clothes on; this guy was a talker.

Sometimes sex was easier. Four years before, I'd have taken a talker anytime, but my solitude had become more valuable than my sexuality. One of my first clients had been at the Clift Hotel, a wizened Irish dwarf who'd had me believe he was an IRA terrorist. Six hours of blarney and a few fifths of Jamison's was a fine way to make a living—and he never touched me. Times had changed; I'd hardened with the drugs. I didn't have six hours to spend with the little people, and a quick sniff of heroin took me way beyond the warm delirium of whiskey. I was striving to get to a nowhere beyond all the pathetic needs and desires of myself and these men. I wanted no one-ness, the dark silent beyond of endless consciousness.

Craig was really out there; the tirade against his wife was endless: she was gorgeous; he never cheated on her; they had a daughter whom he worshipped; he bought his wife a BMW; she flew first class; she went sailing with Mick and Jerry and had a private audience with Osho. Craig was perfect, perfect in his love for her and the life he'd made. He'd discovered his wife's imperfection—she was a spoiled, bored wife of an ignorant social-climbing coke king.

"Beautiful girls. The best in the world. I could have any slice of cunt I wanted. And I was true to her! What a fool to trust any fucking bitch. It's what a man lives for, what he works for. To find a girl that he can take care of and do everything for. I made her a queen and she went behind my back doing smack. My wife is a junkie!" Craig caught his breath and switched from the tragic to the vehement octave.

As he began to degrade women in general, I knew his hatred included me, too, but I kept nodding my head, agreeing with him. So his wife had been doing heroin behind his back—everyone in the valley knew she was strung out. He was the last to know. It was the predictable ending to a common story. The big deal was his hurt pride, the deception; his fall from grace was implicit in hers. "Anything but that," he said. "I would've given her anything."

The tragedy of acquiring more power than you had the imagination to use was common in my world. All the big-dreaming, baby-booming hippies and hopefuls who were going to change the world—we'd gambled, we'd won, and we were horrified with the reward. A whole legion of working-class kids with more money, drugs, and ecstasy at their fingertips, and no one had a vision of where to go with it.

As Craig ranted, I thought of the little paper of heroin in my wallet. I knew how it was—no one could refuse this abundance of coke—there was never enough. The most precious commodity in the world and it reduced you to a lunatic, craving more. Deranged, horrible satori. Heroin was the only antidote.

"I had to get rid of her," Craig moaned.

Bastard, I thought, not wanting to know what "get rid of her" meant. I empathized with his wife; we were the same woman now. Of course she did heroin. Of course she deceived him.

"I understand," I said to Craig.

Both of us were so fucked up that our words flew around like disintegrating electric particles. Finally he was silent, sitting on the bed with his head down. He held a razor blade in his hand, dangling between his legs.

"I gotta go Craig."

"Yeah, I know. You're a nice girl," he replied, as I beelined for the stairs. The motherfucker.

I hated men who hated women. I felt poisoned by Craig's misogyny, by his wife's failure, and by the knowledge that I could share her fate. My duplicity would be revealed, all my carefully covered tracks discovered, my rage and hatred and resistance to becoming the object I pretended to be. The thought of being banished from this liminal kingdom—back into the overweight, barfly-on-nowhere job scene made my stomach churn and my head bang. Fuck me if I'd ride the bus, punch the clock, and get fat again.

One of the big candles on the kitchen table had burned out. Colleen had left. Drew was at the kitchen table, a petrified lump, propped on his elbow. I kissed the top of his head; he seemed annoyed.

The first daylight had come in the window, and everyone's sense of humor had vanished. Lauren sat like a bug-eyed statue, half naked, on the floor in front of the cold fireplace. Charlie sat in a chair in front of her with his pants down around his ankles. He got nasty when I said it was time for us to go.

"I haven't come yet," he said angrily. As far as anyone knew, he hadn't come in years. This problem was usually handled delicately.

Lauren wiped her mouth with her hand. She was barely moving. I gathered her things from the floor for her. Drew and Charlie were both up, hovering over Lauren. Edgy. Charlie's dick was hanging out of his fly like an obscene postscript. Suddenly I had to get out.

"I'll be outside," I said. I saw a flash of urgency rush across Lauren's face. She shifted into gear as I ran up the stairs, grabbed a bottle of wine off the table, and took off out the door.

The dawn felt cruel on my brain; the light hurt my eyes. I dropped the bottle of Jardot as I crammed myself into the car—shattered. Fuck. I wished I'd grabbed some quaaludes. My face felt like cardboard, and the rest of my body felt like it belonged to someone else. The world hurt. I wished I could close my eyes forever.

Lauren fell into the passenger seat, a ghost woman. The sound of the engine scared us both. I craved silence; Lauren tore Bob Dylan out of the tape deck. Eat your heart out Bob—go fuck yourself.

At the bottom of the hill, people were going into the 7-Eleven for their morning coffee. People were going to work, and I felt like a nuclear disaster. The sun came out; it was agony to be abroad in the daylight. I panicked. I knew I needed more coke. I felt as if I would die if I came down, and I was terrified of getting stopped. What if I didn't get home to do some more?

"I might as well go to Berkeley with you," said Lauren, who lived in San Rafael. Neither one of us wanted to be alone. The atmosphere in the little car felt close to exploding; our frantic energies repelled each other in the silence.

The ride home was awful, with the sun blaring and the glare bouncing off the Bay. The daylight attacked us from every direction. I parked on the corner of my block. Kids were going to school, and I hated them. All I could focus on was getting to the safety of my apartment. Finally, I unlocked my door and climbed the stairs. The place was cold; I pulled the shades and turned on the heat.

We sounded like dying geese blowing our packed-dry noses, trying to loosen up dehydrated nasal cavities. Our heads ached and felt stuffed with Styrofoam. Noses were definitely not operative.

"Don't you have a rig hidden somewhere?" Lauren asked me. I started to give her a look but cut it short; I was too desperate to get some drugs in me. I went into the walk-in, living-room closet and opened one of the drawers. I took out the cheap, pink jewelry box that my grandmother had given me for Christmas when I was ten. It was full of little pins and rings, my charm bracelets, and baubles collected over the years—nothing I'd be caught dead wearing. I took out a plastic syringe, one of the big-barreled ones with the blue caps, from under an envelope full of photographer's proofs from my teenage, horse show days.

Lauren had revived herself and found a spoon and a glass of water. I put some coke and a dash of dope in the spoon and diluted it with 30 cc's of water, then drew the solution up through a piece of filter torn from a cigarette. Lauren held out her arm, pressing her thumb on her mainline above her elbow; she had fabulous veins. I fixed her. As I pulled the needle out of her arm, she sighed, and her face lit up in a flash of ecstasy. Lauren groaned, closed her eyes, and settled in the chair with her head back against the wall. I loved to see Lauren rush; she absolutely melted into her pleasure, but my own need shrieked.

I rinsed the works out and mixed the same concoction, a little more generously, for myself. My veins were difficult; I had to take my belt off and wrap it around my arm. I went in the bathroom. Sitting on the toilet seat, I stabbed myself three times—that arm was collapsed. Damn! I was shaking. There was blood on my blouse; I ripped it off and tied off my wrist. I got a register in the back of my hand and slammed the plunger down.

The flavor of cocaine filled my mouth, and I rushed hysterically. For a brief moment, I was more alive than any creature on earth. That passed, and a moment of pure terror ensued. There was a roaring like a giant waterfall in my ears. I felt my whole body quake, like I was riding too fast on an incredibly bumpy road. The black and white tiles on the bathroom floor swirled up and filled the room. My vision blurred, and everything went black. Had I done too much?

A little voice alternately screamed and whimpered in my head. Up and down. Something forgotten tried to come through the dark. It was there; I saw it, and I lost it. I was little, and my hands were flying around, looking for something to hold on to. I held on to the toilet paper with my right hand and the sink with my left.

I was on the floor. The toilet paper was in the tub, and the toilet paper holder was ripped out of the wall. The terror returned. I couldn't stand for the rush to end. I was crashing—then the dope kicked in and caught me. Once the heroin hit, I rinsed the rig out and stumbled back into the dining room.

"You okay?" I croaked at Lauren.

"Yeah, man, did you get it?" Lauren mumbled, rolling her head back farther, searching for my vacant eyes with her own. I headed right by Lauren to the bedroom, dropped my jeans on the floor, and fell into the rumpled bed.

Heavenly. The sheets were rumpled and cool, but the comfort was as warm as a beach blanket in some Caribbean paradise, as wholesome as a white, linen tablecloth spread on an opulent, green lawn.

My world was both inside and outside of the rest of the world. It contained all the violence I thought I was hiding from, but it offered the peace of an isolation tank. I could have been in outer space, drifting in hydrogen, brains blown and molecules dispersed. Rocking. Floating. Drifting. Gone. There is no color in my cubicle, no sounds, no pressure. It is clean. Pure. Beyond simple. Painless, perfect nothingness. No god, no angles, no storms, no demands. Before I even put my head down, I am absolved.

TREATS

9

Bodhisattvas Among Us: Compassionate Sex Workers

Nina Hartley

I doubt that many of the thirty thousand men I meet and greet each year ever fathom that I am looking at them as much as they look at me—and I'm usually naked! When they finally meet me in person (some after more than a decade of waiting), they are often too dazed, giddy, dumbfounded, boisterous, or shy to have any serious conversation with me.

There are exceptions, of course (I've had many wonderful conversations with fans over the years), but it remains true that most are not aware of my perception of them. After sixteen years as an adult entertainer, I can now place any fan accurately into one or more of the many categories of fandom. Although there are significant differences among subgroupings, most fans are bound together by one thing: they, almost to a man, are the walking wounded of the gender wars.

They don't often realize that their pain and confusion, ignorance, hope, anger, and longing are obvious to anyone with my experience. Some would be mortified, others relieved, to have their most personal secrets known without having to actually speak them. This transparency makes a fan as vulnerable as a newborn. It is healing to me to practice compassion when confronted with such primal feelings and to reflect back to these men a healthier and saner sexuality so that they can take it home with them and use it to make their lives and relationships a little better. There is great power in dispensing that "balm of Gilead," and that power must be tempered by compassion.

According to *Merriam Webster's Dictionary:* Bodhisattvas are beings that compassionately refrain from entering Nirvana in order to save others.

Being open to their pain and helping to soothe it is greatly aided by my status as a veteran sex professional and registered nurse (RN). Raised in Berkeley, California, the youngest of four children, my parents were middle-class Communist professionals; by the time I was ten, they had metamorphosed into Zen Buddhist refugees, overwhelmed by the trauma of my father's blacklisting. I was raised in a Buddhist household, and my parents remain active in San Francisco's Zen community to this day. I expected to complete college, and I did, earning a Bachelor's of Science in Nursing, magna cum laude, in 1985. I started dancing while attending school full-time. My class and educational background prevented me from feeling or being victimized by others' lack of respect for sex work/workers. I know my value, and my fans' admiration and devotion demonstrate it.

There are many venues where I meet my fans: conventions (where I am scantily dressed); peep booths (where we can both be naked); Polaroid photo sessions (where I can be dressed, topless, or naked); and university classes and on the street (where I am dressed). At each of these places (except the peep booths), they can hug and touch me. This contact is incredibly powerful and intimate, and I cherish it greatly. For the most part, my fans understand and accept that they are probably never going to sleep with me, so the significance of the touching is magnified. I look them in the eye, hug them, and let them hug me and feel my body (within legal limits, that is). I love the physicality, so I caress them as much as possible (ruffle hair, nibble and kiss earlobes, squeeze shoulders, smack their butts, etc.), making tangible my affection and acceptance.

In our repressed, pleasure-phobic culture, people, particularly males, are chronically touch starved. The difference in how we handle male versus female infants is well documented. The connection between the nature of the touch received by babies and how it impacts their future "emotional intelligence" must be acknowledged by society so that we can address it calmly, change our understanding of the role of sex work, and eliminate the laws that criminalize so much of it. It is a sad fact that men generally have few, or no, socially approved nonsexual outlets to experience caring, human(e) contact. For many, this absence of positive touch adds greatly to the growing psychosis of our times and is manifested, in part, by an increase in violence in our culture, especially among the young.

The revolutionary eruption, thirty years ago, of long-suppressed feminine rage and anger that so characterized the early days of the feminist movement also created the culturewide fallout that we are still sorting out today. Many are still reeling from the initial blast: collateral damage includes a wide-scale abandonment of the nurturing of mates, children, and society that is only now beginning to be addressed. In this confused landscape, there are fewer and fewer places where a wounded spirit can seek shelter and comfort, recognition and acceptance. The sex worker can, and does, provide this comfort, whether s/he is aware of it or not, and even when the consumer is unaware that s/he is seeking these things. Sex workers are the medics at the front lines of the gender wars, the Clara Bartons and Florence Nightingales, patching up the troops, reviving their spirits so that they want to live another day. When sex workers are also educated, conscious, and willing, the healing potential increases exponentially. Banded together as part of a larger movement, this potential staggers the imagination. As has been said before, "When prostitutes unite, powerful men tremble."

At clubs across the country where I dance, there are usually one or two women who really like their jobs and, more important, don't resent or hate men for their sexuality. These dancers are drawn to me because they can tell that I am empowered and don't disrespect either the customers or myself. In mentoring these precious few, I let them in on the single biggest secret of live sex performance (particularly dancing): the men don't know it, but they are coming to church. They are seeking absolution, acceptance, understanding, compassion, kindness, and caring from a willing, friendly woman— if she is pretty, so much the better. They believe themselves to be fundamentally unlovable *because* of their sexuality: if women *really knew* what got them off, they would be cast into the void.

Granting these men acceptance and understanding instead of disgust and ridicule is the single most profound aspect of sex work. Reinforcing that understanding with an orgasm is, in my opinion and experience, the most effective way to get this message across permanently. The more a sex worker understands her/his role in both the psyche of the customer and the scheme of the greater society and history, the better s/he can do her/his job. The fringe benefits for her/him are maintaining mental health and building a loyal customer base.

Being a "star," instead of an anonymous worker, I am treated differently by consumers of commodified sex. Media exposure (TV, movies, print, video) has served to make me more visible and to grant me legitimacy in the eyes of many. As a deliberately open sexual woman, people come to me as to a confessor, doctor, or therapist. They tell me very personal and private things with never a thought that I might find it distasteful or might not keep it secret. Their relief at finally being able to simply talk to someone without being judged is palpable. After unburdening themselves, they wait anxiously for my response. That response can make or break someone's self-image, their intimate relations, even their ability to respond sexually (alone or with a partner).

Fans hand over a lot of power to such an "adored one." My code of ethics demands that I honor that and always treat them kindly. My position as a respected "expert" obligates me to keep my ego out of it, to be firm (or even stern), and to urge them to keep working toward wholeness and love. The average person is still like a child when it comes to her/his sexuality. All her/his fears, insecurities, shame, guilt, self-esteem, capacity for joy and love lie jumbled together in an inchoate mass of quivering need; s/he yearns to be known by one wiser, and loved anyway, accepted to the core, if only for a moment.

I provide this service, along with others in my field, willingly: grateful for the opportunity to help my fellow man and satisfied that I can do what I do best. As is true of any effective art, what gives my work resonance is its emotional authenticity. What is wonderful about sex work is its dual reality as both a bona fide healing art and legitimate artistic expression. Sex workers should take pride in the important work they do and the essential service they provide: simple human kindness in time of need. As Buddha said, "What greater wisdom is there than compassion?" I work toward a society that can honor sex work instead of fear it. I work toward a society that will no longer need to commodify sex, one that does not equate sex with evil or debasement. Although I dream that one day people will be able to look to one another for love, support, and community, until that day arrives, sex workers are desperately needed.

–10–

Clocking In

Mariah

Most of my friends in the Village are prostitutes. When I first came out there, I was—not ashamed to say it—but I didn't want everyone to know. But Christopher Street is really close to Fourteenth Street, so when it gets late, we say, "Okay, girls, I'm going to pull a date, suck a dick, make a bill, call a friend, and do it again." Everyone's so funny. We get to Fourteenth Street, and as soon as we hit the sidewalk, we say, "I'm clocking in." All night we have funny arguments, like bitch that's my date. Or, bitch I'm in the union. It hits seven o'clock in the morning, and the sun starts coming up, and we say, "I'm doing overtime."

I got in a car with this old Jewish guy. He told me he just wanted to fuck around; he didn't want to stick anything anywhere. So when I got in the car with him, he paid me the money and told me to start rubbing his chest. I did that, and he started making these weird sounds. Eventually, he got hard; it was noticeable. After about a half hour it was like he was going to have an orgasm and I wasn't even touching his body. I grabbed his ears, and two minutes later he started to come; he said, "How did you know it was my ears that would make me come?" And I didn't know—it was so funny I cracked up laughing.

I was in a car with another trick who told me he wanted to take me to a hotel. I told him no, unless he wanted a double date. He said no and then he locked the doors and gave me money, and I gave him a blow job. He started saying stuff like, "You're not going to leave me. You're staying with me," and I was thinking, he's just saying that, he was in that mood. After he came, I said, "Can you open the

door?" He said, "I don't want to open the door." I told him he was
going to open the door—right the fuck now! He said, "No, I don't
want to let you leave." I said, "You're going to open the door." So
one of my girlfriends came from behind the car and hit the car with
a brick. She said, "Let my girlfriend out." He reached into his
pocket. I thought he was going to get a knife or something, but he
said, "Here's your tip," and he gave me another twenty.

Another guy, from a bread truck, likes me to feed him bread
while I'm jerking him off. This other trick likes to watch two drag
queens suck each other off. I said, "For me to do that, you have to
pay me a lot of money," and he paid me a lot of money. So I have
fun. I enjoy being out there. I have friends, and I laugh all night
because they're so funny, and usually I make a lot of money.

One day this guy came up to me and just handed me forty dollars.
At first, I thought he was a cop. I said, "I'm not taking that fucking
money." My friends told me to take the money, that he was the guy
who went around and paid the girls if they were pretty. So I took
that money quickly. I thought the guy was weird, but then every
time I saw him after that, I tried to look pretty.

I have one guy—his name is Jay—who lives in Queens; he drives
around all night looking, around and around. Then if you're still out
there in the morning, and he likes you, he asks you to come home
with him. Once you get to his house, he wants you to get naked and
tie him up, get him high off of coke and weed. Then he wants you to
beat him, beat him, beat him. He has this liquid in a bottle that you
put in a napkin and stuff it in his face, then he breathes in. He wants
you to put your hand in a big pile of coke and stuff the coke in his
face for him to inhale. I refuse to do that without any gloves because
I'm not getting locked up for anybody. But most of the time, it's
fun—he pays you by the hour, and he can take so much pain; you
beat him with all your might and he just says more. He's the date
that's the most fun—he gets you high, and he likes you to bring
friends; one time he paid me and a friend to watch us fuck.

This one old guy who takes me to a hotel likes me to give him
head, but he can't get hard most of the time. I sit there for an hour
with him, and he doesn't get hard. Last time, I was thinking, "Do
you have any Viagra with you because I don't want to be with you

all night this time. Do I have to go to the corner store and buy some Viagra?"

I met this guy who couldn't speak English very well. He said, "You like big dick? You like big dick?" I said, "I love big dick, yeah Daddy. I like a lot of money too." He opened his wallet and put it near his dick, and I grabbed all the money—acting like I was trying to touch his dick. Now I feel kind of bad about myself, but then I said, "Oh no, the cops!" and I jumped up and ran away without even doing anything.

This one guy keeps all types of dildos in his car. He has a gallon of K-Y jelly. I didn't think they sold it that big, like a factory-size container. He likes you to smack him in the face with a rubber dildo dipped in K-Y and he likes you to put clamps and chains all over his body. He hires two of us at once to go into his minivan; the seats are always out. I wonder what the cops would say if they checked his car and found all those dildos.

The other day, I was on Thirty-fourth Street and this guy tried to be smart. He came up to me and asked, "Didn't I see you on Fourteenth Street last night?" I thought really quick. I knew I'd never seen him before, but I said, "Oh yeah, where's my tip?"

– 11 –

The House I Grew Up In

Brian Pera

It has been said that I'm prone to myth making when it comes to a certain house on the East Side of midtown Manhattan. And it's probably true. But it's equally true that the house and the things that go on in it lend themselves to myth, at the very least, and if there are myths to be made, perhaps it's more fitting they should be made from inside out. I'm speaking of the house otherwise known as the brothel, the whorehouse, the bordello, the Madam's. The house I came to for the first time years ago, what seems like a lifetime and has, in significant ways, been one. The house that inhabits my loose concept of anarchy and family, of belonging on my own terms; that seems steadier than any other home I ever knew, impermeable to change, even though, by the very nature of its profession, it is at best only ultimately transitory. That it has lasted this long is a more spectacular sense of illusion than anything else prostitution could be accused of. And it shows up the hypocrisy of so-called real families, which have withstood much less.

I first heard about the house from Edward, a roommate of mine who'd been working there a year or so. Edward who is himself an illusion, who's now a woman, or looks that way from the outside. Edward who dyed his hair blue and had two-inch metallic blue fingernails affixed to match before he finally decided to go whole hog. He said the madam at the brothel was looking for another cleaning boy, said they only hired gays there, for reasons obvious and not so. Obvious because gay guys are considered a lot of fun to spend your downtime with, though I myself wouldn't want to spend any significant amount of time with most of those I've known. Not

so obvious, I guess, because we would serve as—what—some kind
of protection? Never mind that most of those girls have never needed any, at least not any kind we could provide. More fundamentally,
it was simple logic. Gay guys wouldn't be sexually involved with
the whores.

I hate to focus on my initiation there; it strikes me as so mundane
compared to the wealth of experience that followed. But one of the
things you quickly learn about the house is that people on the outside
are obsessed with getting in, with the act of crossing the threshold,
with discovering the secrets. So it seems relevant that I got lost the
first time I looked for it, despite precise directions. I was told the
address of a certain black door, East Side. I went West. When I called
from the corner, I listened to a patient Madam—her voice battling the
ringing of what sounded like a dozen phones—as she explained the
obvious all over again. Point being, the house submerges, hides
itself, as well as it's designed to; it could have been any building on
that block from one end to the other. It still could be. People inside
sometimes feel precarious, like sitting ducks. Yet the truth is that
people outside are so obsessed primarily because it *is* difficult to
distinguish and even more so to get in; all kinds of barriers—social,
legal, and otherwise—protect against easy access. Getting in is never
less than a challenge, which is probably at least partly why vice cops
act like such triumphant juveniles once they've broken through to the
other side.

The madam told me several things during my interview, chief
among them that my legs would be broken if I ever wrote about the
place and my experiences there. I don't think she even knew I was a
writer. But I didn't know she was serious, so we were even. She
asked what I thought about the place, what I expected out of the job,
what I thought about prostitution. I remember sitting in a room that
looked very much like a normal room, yet couldn't be, unless the
concept of the kind of room it was meant to represent was changed—
unless one was willing to disregard the standards and norms trum-
peted by a culture one never half believed in to begin with, rather
than carry such notions around like dead weight.

I had problems differentiating in the beginning, and it got me into
a lot of trouble. I waltzed right in and made myself at home, without
any sense of measure or careful thought toward the dynamics of

assimilation. In most ways, I was a thoroughly idiotic child, thought the place was my playground—Let's all have some fun. I was the worst kind of john. I wanted to sit around and talk, shoot the shit with my new friends, go out to eat with them, make instant attachments. A textbook definition of enmeshment. Within my first month of working—if you can call what I did anything so formal—I was fired a grand total of three times. I was worse than any hooker they'd ever hired, in the sense that I was disrupting business without simultaneously making them any money.

Part of my job was to run errands—anything from following a john down the street to see where he would go, to buying cases of condoms, Kleenex, and K-Y at the corner drugstore. But I saw these tasks as opportunities to visit our sister whorehouse a few blocks over. One day, not two weeks after I'd been hired, I was asked to make copies of schedule sheets: ever industrious, I thought I'd bring them to the other house and visit with my new girlfriends over there while cutting the sheets the required foursquare. When Madam found out where I was, she called to do some visiting of her own. Fired me, no questions asked. It's truly a testament to just how clueless I was that my feelings were deeply hurt, and that I tried to argue my case during business hours.

Amazingly, she kept me on. But because I liked the other house so much, she sent me over there for good. It was, after all, where all the problem children went. The main house was too much to risk, whereas the sister start-up was something of a lark for the proprietor. A lark that got busted every month or so, before New York had ever heard the word Giuliani. My first day there, the blue shirts showed up on the phone room TV monitor bright and early—stupid fucks didn't realize we had a camera on the sidewalk, so that their melodramatic crouch-prance toward the door gave us plenty of warning time. Some of these girls had never been busted before, which was really the first of many surprises to little old jaded me. (One of the assumptions about female hookers is that they lead lives of hardened crime. Very often, they're putting themselves through law school, and the closest they have been to a jail cell is watching a prime-time cop drama.) I dashed between the monitor and the living room, trying to help six hookers in minis and stilettos look more like law students than stereotypes, covering them with blankets and urging them to pretend they'd had a late-night study session gone slumber party. By the time the cops were in, I was upstairs intently polishing a bedside table in what we called the "Executive Room"—stars and stripes and lawyerly looking stuff—trying to exude cleaning boy more than pimp.

Unfortunately, many of the stereotypes about prostitutes were not so easily or aggressively thwarted at that house. I hated working there. Of four phone girls, one was a heroin addict who nodded off in front of the monitors—crouch-prancing cops be damned—while the other three made no persuasive argument for the legalization of the profession. The girls on the floor were often no better. These were all the rejects from the other house, the ones who sniffed a constant, questionable sniff, whose presence always seemed to coincide with someone's money disappearing. One of them sat in the living room all day discussing the positive merits of Hemingway, debunking—in a matter that involved more denial than theory—the unfair myths about Papa's horrendous attitude toward women in general and prostitutes in particular. A few years later, she got a boob job and a silicone labia injection, hair extensions that looked like she'd pulled stray fabric off a castaway couch, and Lennon glasses—to better facilitate her literary roundtables, I guess. She's hardly even the worst example, just one of the more achingly memorable.

There was no structure there, no rules, and the chaos hardly made up for it in quality excitement. Regardless of what it looked like— and it did at least *look* nice—in spirit it was one flea short of a flophouse. But even the physicality of the place was hard to adjust to, so self-conscious was it of its illusions. Aside from the Executive Room, there were five others, four of them operable; each of the four had a theme and a name to match, from the Ziegfield Room and its framed portrait of Billie Burke to the Captain's Room, with just about everything nautical but seasickness. The place was tacked and stapled and thrown together haphazardly: shutters propped against windows instead of installed, canopies thumbtacked to the ceiling, plastic flowers without even the pretense of a vase. The one reassuring sense of consistency was the fifth room, the spare, which served as storage for whatever girl happened to need it. To me, this redeemed the place somehow, as if, despite everything, the will of some of us to impose our signatures would win out.

All kinds of things happened in one house or the other. I could titillate with the details. I'm funny about it, though. Granted, a lot of it was exceptionally vivid or bizarre, something you'd talk about no matter where it happened. But a lot of it—the majority—was down-right banal. Depending on whom I'm talking to or who's grilling me with questions, I emphasize one or the other. Because the truth is that the house experienced no more scandal, excitement, or intrigue than any other building that breathes from inside with the dynamics of complex habitation by conflicting personalities and circumstances. To insist that it was more exciting, more thrilling, relies on a prurient voyeurism I don't care to aid in perpetuating. I happen to think that the intrigues inside your own house far outdo anything I could tell you about the brothel; you just have everything invested in seeing it as otherwise. The brothel scapegoats nicely, in a way that allows you to believe that no matter what happens in your own domain, there are depraved hookers who live a life far more decadent. This seems, to me, a fairly established process of surrogacy, from the Bible to the Bible Belt, and everywhere in between.

Whenever the sister house was busted, the vice cops came in like boys raiding the enemy camp. They did everything they could to humiliate the whores; if they interrupted a session, they brought the women down naked, whereas the johns they'd been with somehow materialized fully clothed. Those cops used the situation as a way to talk down to women, the perfect opportunity for men whose authority, in the real world, held so little sway anymore with the "girls" with whom they came into contact. Here, they could practically spit on their wives or mothers or the chicks who had rebuffed their advances, make no bones about their contempt, take out on these women a lifetime of manhood's empty promise, the sham of so-called sovereignty and half-baked spiritual leadership. Then they took Polaroids of the women, as is, though one time I did see a cop toss a throw pillow at one of them (how gallant of the conquering hero, never mind that the woman had to extend her arms to catch it, which meant uncovering her breasts for the whole room to see). The johns, though, lined up in the living room with the rest of us, were allowed to leave, with only a slap on the wrist. To me, they embody the luxury people want to enjoy when the question of the brothel comes up—to experience it without consequences or responsibility, no matter who is exploited in the process.

I can only go by my own examples. Yes, it's true that when I first came to the house, I heard nothing but stories about how the madam used to break people's bones, throw furniture in a rage, slap, hit—you name it. I could say it was sick to sit around in the phone room laughing about it, as the girls and I, sometimes nervously, sometimes comfortably, did. I could say that all this says something intrinsic to the nature of prostitution, authority, and so on. But I'd be wasting my time if I didn't mention in the same breath the grandmother I grew up exposed to, if I left out how her seven children sat around the dining room table at every reunion laughing about her tantrums, her hitting sons over the head with rolling pins, throwing pots and pans at fleeing targets. These things don't say shit about prostitution unless you want them to. And making the theories fit involves a lot of careful omission. Prostitution is, simply, like the nuclear family, a vehicle to both embody and shroud larger issues that ultimately might have little to do with it.

I remember the scandalous things, sure—scandalous even for a brothel. And I have my opinions about all of it. I was there. But I'm protective of the people who were there with me. It's for me and them to sit around the table laughing about. I hold these secrets sacred because every step of the way I chose to be there; I keep them because, far from being dirty family secrets, they are the precious stuff my life is made of, and they aren't for sale. Interestingly, few people wish to hear about the things that have most informed my life in regard to the house. In listening to me discuss them, they practically fall asleep—just check out behind their eyes, wondering when the good stuff comes. I must be an impostor, or an idiot; don't I realize where I was and what's truly interesting about it? As if they needed me to tell them the stories they've already written.

More than anything, I remember the sense of structure the house blessed me with, a sense of regularity and sanctity of ritual I'd never had. I'd certainly never been given those things by my real family, which shuffled me around so relentlessly and remorselessly. I grew up without a home—I was what this country produces but can't take responsibility for; I attest to the lie of the suburban domicile, as if it needed another chink to expose its fallacy. Raised between a well-to-do father and a struggling mother and the various houses and husbands in and with whom she lived, pitted against one or the other, as related to the agenda at hand. I was rejected full-out when there happened to be no agenda to observe, which is to say whenever I became a superfluous liability. The rules of my mother's house made me an outcast in my father's, and vice versa. I see now what the movement was; however unstudied, it was one expert arch toward my banishment, and I unwittingly colluded by accepting the basic sentence, even if I loudly disrupted their music every step of the way. I left without even pictures to prove I'd once been there, and I have few ways of reminding myself where I came from. How's that for myths?

Superficially, the house has offered me very little. A place to stay when I needed one, cakes on birthdays, an ear, community, Christmas dinners with thirteen sweet potato pies a shot. Some people—even some girls at the brothel—would laugh at the power such things have over me. Coming to terms with my life has meant facing that not everyone needs these things to the extent I do. Yet, the house is in the habit of helping people enact fantasy, and that extends beyond the johns. Very often, the people who come there are leading some kind of double life: time necessarily stops, which creates a shared sense of altered perception. Add to this the fact that we are the keepers of one another's secrets. One tends to get a little confessional, to take emotional risks in bonding. Prostitution is a big part of the consciousness created at the house, obviously, but it's not the half of it.

I was killing time at a coffee shop when I first felt I had a name for the overriding dynamic of the house. I'd picked up a copy of Genet's *The Screens* at a used bookstore, because fags like me are supposed to like him, and saw on the jacket a quote about "inside and outside" brothels. I called up the madam. Had she heard of this play? Had she heard of these terms? Of course she had; there's a lot she doesn't know, but not about prostitution. Still, to me, the information was the portal to a new consciousness. It gave me the sense that someone else had been here, that, yes, maybe the house existed in its own void in many ways, but in just as many it had a unifying history. It wasn't simply something transgressive, but transcendental. After that, I gradually came to understand that what went on inside the house was a microcosm, a highly concentrated reality, of the world at large. Our inside mimicked their outside and, at the same time, necessarily removed us from a sense of continuum. It was that removal that created intimacy. Things seemed to stop inside, not just because of the specific circumstances of the house, but for reasons that had to do historically with prostitution in general and the inside life of outsiderhood.

Eventually, I faced the choice between staying in New York City and moving to Memphis. I visited the city of dead Elvis for a couple weeks and called the madam from there a night before I was supposed to come back. I felt like I'd grown up a little, enough to see that if I ever wanted to actualize myself, I had to move out of New York City and the life I led there. I can't explain to you why it mattered to me what she thought, why I was nervous to tell her I was thinking about moving, as crazy as it sounded. And I can't explain what it meant to me when, rather than getting angry, flying into one of her famed "rages," she expressed nothing but support and encouragement. Ever since I moved to Memphis, she's been my biggest fan. She's been the first person I call whenever anything momentous happens in my life. A trip to New York is a trip to see her and the house, where I can get the feeling no other place gives me—that I'm understood, that a certain level of bullshit is suspended, that the frenetic transiency I'm learning is adulthood can be counteracted by an untouchable strain of spiritual permanency. I know it's a lot to ask of a brothel or anything else, but the house has more than enough sustained that myth.

A year after I left, Edward moved into the fifth room of the sister house and made it his own. People were always living at one or the other. The basement of the main house has hosted some of the city's more memorable, if undiscovered, characters. Edward was only there a few months before a newly instated Giuliani sent a special vice van over to close it down for good. A friend sent me a *New York Post* clipping with a picture of one of the girls leaving the front door, her coat over her head. But I'd recognize that shape anywhere. Stranger than seeing the inside of the house brought out in such a stark way was the prospect of this part of my family life taking such an abrupt turn. Selfish, to be sure. And absurd, considering there had never been any love lost between me and that particular location. But it spoke of change, and the house is the one area of my life where I have the hardest time accepting such things. The story of New York City prostitution in the 1990s has been co-written by Giuliani and Walt Disney, with predictable results. It has forced the surviving house to go further underground, deeper inside, which has, in turn, intensified the sense of camaraderie there and the time warp in unexpected ways. It has even transformed the dynamic between prostitute and john, which often seemed to have been etched in stone.

It's even harder to get in now. Clients are given out codes that are strictly enforced. New members must be referred by regular, trusted johns. There's not as much money to be made this way, as the profession relies on new faces and whim, indeed, as a counteraction against the rut of overregularity. The johns who persist are often as concerned about exposure as the women they see, and the women themselves have usually come to this house in particular for the fact that it's never been busted and neither have they. These factors create a certain mutual conscientiousness that other houses, including the extinct sister house, often don't concern themselves with. Because there are fewer clients, there is more sitting around in the phone room, deeper conversation with fewer interruptions. Granted, this is much to the displeasure of more than a few girls there, but they wouldn't be there if they didn't ultimately appreciate the safety that enables these circumstances.

I've talked about things in that phone room over the last three years that I haven't discussed to the same degree anywhere else or with anyone else in my life. Because nothing is sacred, everything is. I was able to discuss my own experience in prostitution (for which I had always been given demos no real-time family would ever dare engage in, and which therefore gave me more protection and the esteem to use it), and see the trajectory between all sex work, the relationships I found myself in, and more basically, I was allowed to just—finally—kind of shoot the shit, now that I'd earned insider status. The house has given me place and identity, ironically; imagine, in such a scattershot culture, and from such a quintessentially transient profession, I've somehow extracted permanency.

The house has, in every conceivable way, had a hand in shaping who I am, which is why I now find myself writing about it.

The madam sent me off to Memphis with two hundred bucks, her home phone number (which only a few people at the brothel have ever been given), and the assurance that, "Out of all of us, you'll be the one to publish." No one else in my life had ever given me such support, and however blind it was, however steeped in motherly denial, it's given me an equally blind ambition. Four years later, I completed a book, and an editor was considering it. I'd never half-believed the madam right; I just wanted to make good on her confidence. Unfortunately, it dawned on me that what had been a private story—something I never really thought would be made public—revealed parts of my life at the brothel, even if metaphorically. The dilemma I faced had nothing to do with a fear of my legs being broken, as the madam once promised. Far worse: I was scared shitless that I'd lose the only family I'd ever known.

I took a trip to New York to discuss my dilemma with her. Predictably, she flew off the handle. How dare I write about something I knew nothing about. I was ready, believe me, to pack my bags, to burn both the novel and my bridges. But, to my surprise, she calmed and told me I had every right in the world. "This is your background," she said, "and you have to write about what you know." Leave it to a fellow writer to uphold this myth. Still, despite her blessing, she has yet to read the book—which is what makes it so much more profound that she has been its primary champion.

I should probably say something about Edward, who no longer wishes to be recognized as such. That would be fine in itself; I would gladly respect his illusions if he showed the same for mine. What makes this difficult, and what seems typical of the gay community's search for identity and spirituality at this point, is his renunciation of his past, including the brothel. The Lord has accepted him as her, so she has denounced all else. God saved Edwina from AIDS, she has said, so Edwina now drags her ass to Bible study, where her fellow students accept her despite the titillating details of her questionable past and her ambiguous present. Everything will be fine with her new-won acceptance, if she keeps her mouth shut about certain things, which is to say, everything that matters. She's no different than they are, she assures them—not on the inside.

How characteristic of gay men at this point, regardless of how they define themselves. I never thought, entering the brothel that first day, that I, too, would renounce gay men in my own fashion. But it's been a struggle from the beginning, and the brothel was bound to win. I've had enough talks in the phone room of the brothel to recognize that what the current "gay community" passes off as frank sexual discussion is nothing of the sort, not nearly. I resent that I've been able to talk to these women at the brothel, who've obviously never had gay male sex, about my sex life more openly and with less fear of rejection or veiled prurience than with any gay man. In the increasingly mainstreamed gay community, discourse is structured first and foremost by personality, fueled by egomania—sham and shame based. As slick as Disney's Times Square, and no more satisfying a place to be.

Any so-called oppressed group worth its salt knows that a stifled dialogue about its issues is no dialogue at all; any halfway decent minority sees propaganda for what it is, knows that propaganda seeps up through the roots to poison the plant. In the house, I rarely see the kind of cutthroat exclusionism that propaganda requires. The circumstances don't tolerate it. And because I've been exposed to the house, I don't either. I'm not about to renounce what Edwina has, not for something as flimsy as a consumer-based unity, let alone the Puritanism of a Bible study group.

It seems to me now more important than ever to discuss one's experiences frankly, not to shock, but—to the contrary—to assert. The myths of family and place I've created and sustained at the brothel seem no more tenuous than the falsehoods of suburbia and modern assimilationism. To me, they seem to have more integrity, though perhaps, admittedly, this is just my imagination. Still, the house has always allowed me that. The best myth of all.

Numbers

Jill Nagle

So there I was, a pretty girl with a boner for boy whores, in Los Angeles for the weekend with illustrious hos Lex and River. They told me I had to visit Numbers, a hustler bar some think was named for John Rechy's novel of the same name, whose other novel, *City of Night*, deals with male prostitution. Both novels treat man-on-man sex (both the free and paid varieties) in some depth.

At the time of this writing, Numbers' main door was in a parking lot, next to a deli and a comedy club, completely invisible from the street. This hidden opening gave the act of entering a rather furtive feel, which heightened my excitement. By the time this story comes out, Numbers will have moved to a more public area, which locals believe will change the nature of the bar from primarily a place to turn tricks to a more generic cruising environment in the heart of West Hollywood. This made me sad to hear, and all the more determined to make it to Numbers before the change.

On my last visit, I had met quite a few lovely boy whores, some of whom were bisexual, or at least open. I didn't follow up on any of my contacts because I had a date with a red-hot dyke later that night, and even the bar's best offerings couldn't hold a candle (or any other phallic object, for that matter) to her.

This time, however, I had the night free and went with the intention of either (a) engineering a paid threesome with a bisexual boy whore and a client, or (b) engendering some unpaid dalliance of my own with the fancy-striking sex object of my choice. I wasn't tied to any particular outcome, just open and curious and interested in cruising and being cruised.

River and I spent a few moments at the front of the bar chatting with Lex and his new friend Mark, then headed toward the back to make the rounds. The bar was lined with mirrors and filled with lots of buff young hunks, and also a good number of elderly gents. In most cases, it was easy to distinguish the supply from the demand.

Once in the back, River and I smelled smoke from the rear entrance and began to make our way forward again. But not before I caught the eye of a strikingly handsome gentleman, in his late thirties (which I prefer to the twenties set), with dark hair, a black tank top and snugly fitting jeans, showing off a generous fist-sized basket of goods. I stopped in my tracks and administered my best cruising stare. He looked back, but without enough energy or interest to convince me to return and talk to him. I looked at River and kept moving slowly forward.

"Did you see that?!" I muttered to River.

"Well, go back and talk to him!" River admonished in his thick don't-bother-me-with-your-problems Brooklyn drawl.

"He's probably a Kinsey NINE!" I whined, failing to conjure up the usual chutzpah that would allow me to traverse such trivialities. I followed River back to the front, and we sat in a circular booth, which was ideal, because it allowed us to observe lots of activity and, at the same time, be ready to offer any compelling passersby a seat at our table.

River and I shared woes over champagne and introduced ourselves to our neighbors. We met Daniel, a very handsome young man whose eye I had caught on the way down to the end of the bar the first time, and his androgynous, long-haired, five-o'clock-shadowed friend Leslie. Daniel, it turned out, was straight, and hell-bent on, well, going dancing. He also seemed interested in me. I was only slightly drawn to him, though he was certifiably cute.

As Daniel got up to leave, he was intercepted by a thin, short, bald, midfiftyish-looking guy whom I overheard offering him "a thousand." Daniel was no whore, and my guess was that the idea of servicing this man, for any amount of money, was beyond his reach. But what if I were to come along? I suggested to Daniel that if— what was his name—Roy—if Roy were willing to hire me, too, it might be more fun for everyone (and, of course, lucrative for yours truly).

Meanwhile, River had gone off in pursuit of greener, crisper pastures. His seat didn't stay vacant for long. "Hi there!" said a bulky orange man with too much goop in his tinted blond pageboy, sitting down near me where River had been. His handlebar mustache was at least an inch tall, and a big boxy leather jacket encased his barrel chest.

"Uh, hi." I moved closer to Daniel, exchanging mild flirtations and phone numbers.

"You sure you can't swing this?" I asked Daniel. Roy returned, to instigate a second round of badgering.

"Hey," Roy called to me. "Would you be into a gang bang?"

"With who?" I asked warily. He pointed to Handlebar next to me and a couple of other equally appealing specimens.

"Sure!" I smiled from ear to ear. "For five hundred per guy." Roy balked.

"Well, how about we negotiate?"

"Nope!" I said cheerfully. "That's my price."

"Well, you know, I got this girl who's really into the whole gang bang thing; she really gets into it. I have a great apartment, and a big-screen TV, and she only charges me fifty dollars, you know—"

"Yeah, and?" I interrupted him.

"Well, I just thought maybe you—"

"You know my terms. If you want to do business with me, you know where to find me." I turned from Roy to finish my conversation with Daniel, who was getting increasingly excited about the idea of going dancing and tried to talk me into it. I declined. Daniel and the long-haired Leslie sauntered off into LA partyland, leaving Handlebar and me alone momentarily.

"I've never been with a woman," he said brightly, with a smile that was too eager. I raised an eyebrow.

"You don't believe that?" he asked.

"I'd believe you've never been with a man," I replied, looking off toward the rear of the bar, directly into the eyes of my beloved Basket. "Hey!" I called in his direction, newly emboldened by the champagne. "My name's T. J. Would you like to sit down?" "Sure," he replied, joining us. Roy returned and greeted Basket, who appeared to recognize Roy. River also returned, having come up empty. Handlebar excused himself, and River resumed his position.

"Do you know Roy?" I asked Basket.

"I've been with him a number of times. He's . . . a little weird. I'm just not in the mood for him tonight."

"Weird like how?" I asked.

"Not dangerous or anything. Just quirky. Annoying. Demanding. But he always backs off if you tell him to. Always."

It turned out that Basket's name (for the evening, anyway) was Troy, and he had starred in over five hundred adult films. He and River began networking about the adult industry, while I commenced a deep meditation on what his nipples looked like, how hard I might be able to suck on them, how his pecs curved out from his chest, how his love trail disappeared into his basket. . . . I was just getting to the tilt of his erection when the subject of exactly what I was doing there came up.

"Are you a writer or . . . something?" he asked perkily.

"Of sorts," I muttered.

"Or something," River snickered.

Earlier, someone I passed had pointed after me and shouted, "Manhattan—writer!" I am so over being seen for only my brain.

Disgruntled, I removed my nerdy glasses, undid my hair, and pulled off my jacket, revealing the upper half of a black lace bustier, discreetly covering and lifting my perky orange-sized breasts a good couple of inches away from where they'd normally land.

"Oh, my," said Troy, blushing slightly.

"Do you like girls at all?" I hazarded. He smiled, answering to my chest.

"Oh, sure. I have girlfriends from time to time. But I'm mainly into guys." Perfect, I thought. Boyfriends were not on the shopping list. And I could stand to watch some hot faggot action tonight.

The crowd in front of the table shifted once again, and we found ourselves faced with Tad, an elfin lad who appeared barely twenty, with a cherubic mouth, and Teran, a taller, muscular, caramel-skinned African-American man with a dazzling smile. Something happened, and the four of us started behaving like a quartet.

"I could be up for an orgy!" Teran offered, playfully.

"Troy, Tad, Teran, and T. J. It's just too, too . . ." I observed.

". . . titillating!" Troy finished.

Tad and Teran, it turned out, were card-carrying bisexuals who were ready to throw back in the trick towel for some trollopy treats.

"Hey," I said, ever enterprising, "why don't we get Roy to foot the bill?" It turns out all of them had been with Roy before, and, I would find out later, River had, during his brief sojourn, given Roy a lecture on how you have to shell out for girl whores; girls don't bargain like boys, he'd warned.

I found Roy and flagged him down.

"Roy," I said, "I will do a gang bang for three hundred dollars flat, *provided*," I paused, "I get to pick the team."

"Well, who do you want?" he asked.

"I want him, and him, and him," I said, pointing at Tad, Teran, and Troy. "And *not* him." I pointed at Handlebar.

"Well, what will they charge?" he asked.

"You'll have to work that out with them," I replied.

A half hour and some convoluted negotiations later, the five of us wound up in Roy's condo.

Roy's high-rise condo featured a big-screen TV facing a king-size bed. To the right of the bed, as you walked in, was a large bathroom, and to the left, a balcony. In addition to Tad, Teran, Troy, and I, Roy had a big, hunky, football-player-sized "housemate" who apparently was in the process of renting some female entertainment of his own that evening. Whispered rumors flew that the "housemate" was actually a kept lover on the way out.

While I lounged on the bed, watching porn, the six of them trotted back and forth behind the big screen, to the kitchen for drinks, the bathroom to snort coke, and the balcony to smoke weed, and back again. It seemed like a chaotic fraternity house.

Roy began laying out an assortment of dildoes in order of size, including one horse-sized one that wasn't really a dildo, but rather a sort of sleeve one slipped on over one's own dick. Roy fished his limp dick out of his shorts and donned the appendage, talking to himself all the while. He positioned himself in the line of traffic, and when one of the guys walked by, he would catch him, turn him around, and start bumping the bewildered lad's bum with his plastic dong.

When one guy escaped, Roy would grab another. By this time, some of them had stripped bare. As the collective level of intoxication increased, the back-and-forth activity kept up, but the level of coordination fell. People began colliding with one another, and Roy was now lunging for, and missing, the butt holes toward which he aimed. When he tried feebly to poke the giant phallus into the deep, dry crack between Teran's melonlike ass cheeks, it was all I could do not to burst out laughing. At one point, I got up, and Roy began careening toward me. I easily maneuvered away, like a toreador dodging a dying bull in the final round of the fight.

Now, as I mentioned earlier, I have had a boy whore fetish for a number of years. That is, the idea of hot young men proffering their sexual services for money gives me a big boner. However, this particular scenario was just about the furthest thing from erotic I could imagine. I was slightly turned on watching the faceless woman on the big screen get fucked from behind, particularly by her clit, which protruded from her lovely pussy. I imagined attending to her clit myself while she continued to get fucked.

The clock was advancing, and I was getting impatient with the bumbling would-be orgyites. I decided (a) to stay no longer than the hour I had promised in exchange for the three Ben Franklins tucked safely in my backpack, and (b) to get fucked by one of the lovely bi boys I had lured into this disorganized lair. It was time to make the king-size bed, where I lay alone, the focus of attention.

My writhing and moaning attracted Teran, whose lovely, smooth hunky body I stroked, licked, and bit with delight. He was soon followed by Tad, whose completely vertical, baseball-bat-like boner grazed his skinny midsection from the moment he dropped his pants. The combination of Tad's boylike face, complete with wide eyes and protruding ears, and his eager dick, made him my target. Troy sat on the sidelines nursing a reluctant penis, providing a running commentary. Roy at first hovered around the outside like a mosquito, looking for an opportunity to pounce with his prosthetic prick, but we shooed him away.

I ripped open an extra-large-sized condom and rolled it onto Tad's quivering member. He moaned as I took him as far down my throat as I could manage. I greased up my pussy, looked at Tad's sweet, happy face and asked, gratuitously, "Would you like to fuck me?" His eyes got even wider as he shook his head up and down, squeezing his beautiful dick. This made it all worth it.

"Can I fuck you while you fuck her?" Teran asked. Tad looked back at Teran and nodded. This was even better, as long as Teran didn't disrupt Tad's rhythm.

Soon, we were all in place and rocking merrily away. Tad's sweet dick inside me was heaven, and his skin smelled like clean laundry, with just a hint of fresh sweat. I kissed his fleshy lips and pinched his hard little nipples.

Roy began making loud, appreciative noises.

"Yeah! Oh, yeah, that's hot! Yeah, go, oh, yeah!" Okay, so Roy knows hot stuff when he sees it. Maybe all this group needed was a little focus. I was suddenly glad for all my group facilitation training.

Tad's dick soon brought me to a delicious edge, and I came hard, spasming again and again under the two beautiful boy whores I had picked up at Numbers. While I was recovering, I noticed that Roy was still murmuring in appreciation, but we were not the source—his eyes had apparently been glued to his big-screen TV the whole time. He had missed the entire show, which, I calculated—between drugs, alcohol, and whore fees—had cost him well over a grand. Tad was still hard, poor dear, but I figured Teran would take care of him. Having had my big bang, and the hour just finishing, I jumped up, thanked them all, took my money and clothes, and wished them all a good night.

Lex and River laughed and laughed and laughed when I told them that part. "You *are* a fag!" Lex marveled. Funny, I hadn't even thought about that part of it. It was the rest of the story that removed any residual doubt about my fag identity; the only female in the joint, I had gone to LA's premier hustler bar with two of the biggest, cutest male hookers in the city. I got work, and they didn't.

–13–

Joel

Kowalski

It was early November when Joel and I had our first session. Months before, his doctor had told him that he would not live through the end of the year. Yes, he had AIDS, but more immediately pressing was his terminal liver cancer.

I ring doorbell number seven, bzzzzzz . . . press open the glass lobby door and climb the stairs to the third floor. A friendly, somewhat frail man, looking older than his fifty-seven years, opens the door and invites me in. Joel is about 5′8″, with a balding crew cut, a strong, deep baritone voice, and big blue eyes hiding behind large, tinted, aviator bifocals. In the small hallway, he takes my jacket and hangs it on the coatrack. We speak of the weather and my bus ride to his hilltop neighborhood as he escorts me into the living room and offers me a seat and a drink. The room contains two seating areas: one a sofa and armchair, where I sit, and the other a TV and a lone armchair surrounded with a matching footstool, a floor lamp, a side table with a pack of cigarettes and an ashtray, a glass with melting ice, an eyeglass case, and balanced on the armrest are three remote controls. Joel returns, brings me my juice, and sits down . . . where he always does . . . in *his* chair on the other side of the room. He's ten feet away from me. So I stand up, walk over, and set my drink down on the table next to Joel, walk back, and as I would come to do regularly, I drag my armchair across the room.

Our sessions developed a routine right from the beginning. I'd arrive, my jacket would go on the coatrack. Sit in the living room, glass of juice, conversation. Sex in the bedroom. Then I'd shower and return to the living room to talk. It wasn't as cold or mechanical as it may sound. It was actually quite intimate. Sex definitely had its importance, but we spent more time talking. The obvious topic, staring us in the face, was death, and it *was,* at times, the topic of our conversation. Of course, sometimes we were talking about death or talking around death and didn't realize it.

When Joel spoke of death and wondered what it would be like, his tone was calm and accepting. He expressed that he was in no hurry. He liked the idea of showing up his doctor's expectation of not surviving into the new year. He talked about his four kids from when he was married, three boys and a girl, grown up now. Joel had come out in his early forties. He told me stories about his kids' childhood. In one, his youngest son, about fifteen at the time, was picked up by one of Joel's friends as a street hustler. It wasn't until the friend was driving with the boy in his car that he recognized him and ended the, uh, transaction. Joel also spoke of conversations he had with his children about his nearing death. He was again calm when he spoke of this and seemed clear, although he had concerns about how his daughter would handle his death. She was having feelings, and this worried Joel. It seemed to me that if she was *having* feelings over her father's nearing death then she was probably dealing with the situation, whereas Joel's emotions tended to be secondary to his thoughts. Of all our conversation topics and all that we shared, what Joel showed the most emotion over, the most enthusiasm over, was me.

After sitting a while in the living room, sipping this week's juice choice, purchased along with the rest of the groceries by the AIDS volunteer, Joel would propose that we go to the bedroom. The room was pretty basic, a queen-size bed with a bookshelf headboard and a pair of dressers. Everything was low, black lacquer with a little chrome trim—very 1979. Authentic. We'd walk in together and begin to undress. I would see to it that I would undress slower than Joel so that he could watch me finish undressing. I wanted to build some erotic excitement. I also didn't want to be standing around waiting with my hands in my pockets, because at that point, pockets would be something I wouldn't have. I was the object here, and it was fun to share that with Joel and play with it.

I take off my shirt and then my boots and socks, pop open the buttons of my jeans, and let my jeans drop to the carpet. Standing there in my briefs, I step out of my jeans. When receiving a gift, it's fun to have something to unwrap. By this time, Joel is lying down or sitting on the side of the bed, wearing his black jock strap. I walk over and stand in front of him, putting my hands on his shoulders and on the back of his neck. He caresses my butt as he nuzzles my dick through my briefs. One of his hands makes its way to one of my nipples as his other hand joins his mouth on my dick. Joel drags my briefs over my butt and down my legs as his mouth finds my half-hard dick. Joel sucks my dick as he holds onto my ass with both hands. I stroke his head and neck, shoulders and back as I feel his wet mouth pass up and down as I get hard. I reach down and find his nipples and flick. Joel moans. I begin to squeeze gently. With each pass, his upper teeth lightly graze the top of my dick. Joel scoots back onto the bed. I climb in and sit with my legs spread. Joel crawls between them and continues on my dick, his hands playing with my balls. My hands caress his head and rest on the sides of his face. Joel plays with his dick in his jock as his mouth licks its way up my torso to find a nipple. Joel strokes his dick as my hand begins stroking my own. I wrap my other arm around his head, cradling him. My breath becomes deeper and Joel continues on my nipple as he looks down at my dick to watch. I wrap my arm tighter around Joel as I jack off. My load shoots onto my chest. I milk my dick as I feel my climax pass over my body. Then I find one of Joel's nipples. Quickly Joel shoots into his jock and into the sheet. We lie there a while, my arm around Joel. Silent.

Then. Slowly. A comment. A sentence. A line or two. A laugh. Joel pulls the covers over us as he lies next to me. Conversation begins. The weather. Current events. My body. His dead boyfriend. The French woman who grocery shops for him. Plans for Christmas. Joel gets out of bed, puts on his robe, and goes to the living room. I get out of bed and go to the peach-and-black-tiled bathroom to shower. Afterward, I return to the bedroom to collect my clothes. Joel has left my fee on one of the dressers. I bring my clothes into the living room to dress while talking to Joel. We talk. We talk about food. We talk about Beavis and Butthead. We talk about my underwear. We talk about my boots. Joel likes my boots. He asks me where I bought them. We talk about their weight and comfort, about the extra protection they offer. We talk about how tough they look, how masculine, how butch. A session or two later, I arrive and Joel is wearing the same boots. He's happy. He proudly shows them off. Talks about his experience purchasing them. How heavy they are. In fact, they're so heavy Joel explains that he can't wear them outside of the apartment. That would be too exhausting for him. Now, each visit, I sit in the living room talking with Joel and he's wearing his boots. Time continues to pass, as does the new year. And January. We continue our sessions. We continue sex. We continue our conversations. February passes.

Joel wants to take me on a trip. At first, when he mentions the idea, he delivers it flirtatiously, only half serious. After a few more sessions, he is quite serious and specifically proposes a train trip to Las Vegas. The accommodations are generous and the demands on me minimal. What Joel asks is that each evening we have dinner together. Out of honor and respect, I agree to think about it and give him an answer at our next session.

I already know what I want. No, thank you. I enjoy Joel for a few hours at a time, but day after day I would feel trapped. At the same time, I want to take Joel's needs and desires into account. So here I am sitting with the ability to grant a dying man a wish. The opportunity to wield the power of wish granting is seductive. I give the offer some thought. A great deal of thought. I decide that it wouldn't be fair to myself to spend time with Joel in a way that I don't want. And that it wouldn't be fair to Joel to spend time with him when I don't want to be there, no matter how much he wants it. I'm not looking forward to telling Joel. The next session, I arrive, jacket on the coatrack. Living room, glass of juice, talk. Bedroom, sex. Shower, return to the living room, conversation. We have been talking in the living room for a while and still Joel hasn't brought up the trip. I know he hasn't forgotten. He's avoiding the topic, perhaps afraid of my answer. This makes it even more difficult. I bring up the topic. I don't drag it out. I get to the point. Joel's response is that he didn't expect me to accept. The exchange highlights the containment of our relationship. Our intimacy is able to be shared within the time of our sessions. Our conversation continues. March passes. I finish my juice. I drag my armchair back to its position. April passes.

Early on, Joel had begun offering me a robe to wear after my shower for our conversation in the living room. This robe became part of our routine. Shower, robe, conversation. After a while, Joel mentioned that he wanted me to have this robe, but I shouldn't take it with me *this* visit because he wanted to have it cleaned first. Of course, at the end of the next visit, again I didn't take the robe with me. Nor the next visit. Nor the next. The robe hadn't gone to the cleaners yet. I assume it never did. Who'd want to acknowledge that this could be our last visit?

– 14 –

Toward a Taxonomy of Tricks: A Whore Considers the Age-Old Question, "What Do Clients Want?"

Carol Queen

Sometimes I wonder what the clients would do if there were no sex workers for them to call when the urge manifests, the fantasy surfaces, the dick throbs, the desire for adventure or connection won't be ignored; or when boredom strikes, and sex seems like the best way to alleviate it.

Would they just live without blow jobs and fingers up their butts? Would they try to get their wives to talk dirty or wear black stockings? Fantasize that their boyfriends are rough trade? What would become of their desires? Would they learn to negotiate for them at home? Look for a mistress or a trophy boy? Close their eyes tight and fantasize hard while they jerk off? Are they right that their wives don't want to do things, or have they simply not got what it takes to make their wives feel wild—like classy whores themselves?

It's a good thing we are here for the johns, whether their bedrooms at home are empty or whether they just feel that way. The johns need the whores' touch. We make them feel safe enough to drop their pants and talk about what they want. To hear a lot of them tell it, they can't do that anywhere else.

Of all the things that make whoring the world's oldest profession, surely the most basic is the commodified desire of the client. Much is said about the economic need that leads people to whoring. I won't contradict that; I've never met a whore for whom money was

105

irrelevant. But for all the talk of "selling our bodies" (which is ridiculous; we still have our bodies at the end of the transaction), the commodification of our time, our flesh, our actions, there's surprisingly little corresponding talk about the client's body, the client's role.

When I say "client's role," I emphatically do not mean client as abuser: this is the first assumption of people who believe sex (at least when exchanged for money) is automatically abusive. This is not my experience at all; in fact, I've experienced many clients as much more pleasant and respectful than a lot of people in my past who wanted to have sex for free. Portraying all johns as abusive is like overlooking the difference between a bank customer and a bank robber because both stand at the same teller's window and make a withdrawal. Equating the purchase of sexual entertainment with abuse or misogyny is too simple, for one thing. It erases useful-to-consider differences between men who are hateful and those who are respectful, and it undermines the client's own experience as well as his motivation for treating whores with respect.

Aside from this specious problematization of the client, it seems to me that the client is not problematized enough—at least, not by society as a whole. Compared to the scrutiny aimed at prostitutes, there has been a reluctance to look closely at the client, his part in the transaction, and his motives. This may be in deference to the many clients who are powerful men, or because so many of them are our husbands and fathers. Their very visibility and proximity act as a veil. Middle-class women, in particular, the ones who tend to be so uneasy about prostitution, don't want to look at their husbands as johns—though whores know better.

The reason the client pays for erotic entertainment is treated as simple: men just want sex. Isn't that natural? We tell ourselves so, whether we code that desire as neutral, negative, or positive. But not all clients want the same things, nor do they want them for the same reasons.

I'd like to explore this, but first I want to say a bit about my position in this discussion. By the way, I will almost always refer to clients as men; most of them are. Whoredom is more gender-integrated, by far, than clienthood.

I have written elsewhere about my experiences in the sex industry, so I'll be brief here. For the better part of five years, all or a substantial portion of my income was derived from prostitution (in call/out call, working with a madam) and/or peep show work. I am mostly retired from prostitution now, although I stay active in the sex workers' community and movement. I never whored full-time, never on the streets, and never had to advertise and engage in aggressive client screening. As an educated woman who entered the industry when I was over thirty, largely protected from both police and bad tricks because all my clients came by referral, I lived about as ideal a whore's life as can be done in a culture that still stigmatizes whores and sex. I was always out as a whore, at least to my partner and my immediate circle of friends, and I live in one of the world's most sex-positive communities. Just as important, I had already lived a queer, unorthodox life and am comfortable identifying as a sexual outsider. Doing so has no negative effect on my self-image, and I understand sexual difference (including whoring) in political terms. All these things influenced the way I worked, how I experienced it, and the interpretation and meaning I draw from it.

My johns were mostly upper-middle-class professional men, ages thirty-five and older—"yuppies and their dads." They were lawyers and insurance executives, physicians and venture capitalists, well-to-do retirees and business owners, stockbrokers and more lawyers. Only a handful were lower-middle-class or young. Most were married, and most were white. They had made it into my madam's "little black book" by being decent (or downright good) clients.

At the peep show, I saw more class and racial diversity by far, and a wider age range: from just barely old enough guys with skateboards to shuffling great-grandpas from nearby Chinatown. Hundreds of men (and a brave handful of women) passed before me in the year I worked there. They came to masturbate (usually) and watch (always) and sometimes to talk—about their lives and especially about their fantasy lives. A pane of glass separated me from my customers there, a separation that seemed to make men willing to reveal more of their inner sex lives, since skin-to-skin contact was not available to bridge the gap between us.

I became a prostitute for the same reason nearly all of us do: for the money. But I stayed at it partly because I was curious about the men, fascinated by their stories and the accommodations the sex industry allowed them to make for their sexualities. I wondered (and still do) what differentiates them from men who do not desire or allow themselves to patronize the sex industry, and how the sex they have with me and my colleagues compares to the kind of sex they have (or would like to have) at home. I wonder, too, especially in this time of increasing legal attacks against both johns and prostitutes, how so many of them manage to understand their experiences with whores in such a depoliticized context. Or, to put it another way, if all men are really johns, you'd think there'd be more guys out protesting as cops in one jurisdiction after another impound clients' cars as punishment for the crime of putting dollars in whores' pockets. You'd almost think the cops and politicians want all the whores for themselves.

So, to be clear as to my relationship to clients and to sex work in general: whether or not all men are clients, and whether or not more women gradually join the men who already comprise the over-whelming majority of our client base, I believe everyone has the right to sexual connection and pleasure. The men who pay for play are exercising that right, and I believe it's as wrongheaded for sex workers and the sex-positive community to ignore the issues of johns as it is for, say, feminists to ignore the issues of sex workers. That said, I neither deny nor excuse the presence of abusive cli-ents—but I *do* think that for every abusive client, there are many others who play the game fairly.

So—what do clients want? Blow jobs—but you already knew that. Here I want to expound on the most common agendas I saw in my clients. Thinking about this in some detail shines a light on the sexuality of the mainstream, since so many clients are fundamental-ly "ordinary" men. What follows is a breakdown of client motiva-tion, as I've seen it.

Convenience—that is, men see prostitutes because they can. The sex industry exists to get guys laid (at least, it holds out the promise of doing so). Clients who've figured out how to work the system (who've learned where sex workers are, how to contact them, and how to relate effectively to them) know that sex can be scheduled and arranged almost as easily as ordering takeout. For certain clients, being able to schedule sex, even when it means booking time with a professional, beats every alternative. These are the yuppies who, when I wasn't available within a certain twenty-minute window of opportunity, would hardly bother to pretend they'd find a more convenient time later. ("Maybe I'll catch you some other time," they'd say, then hang up to dial another number.)

Related to the "my-time-is-valuable" phenomenon (which tended to make the guys accept that my time was valuable, too) is the "meeting-people-wastes-time" phenomenon. I realize that many outsiders to the industry hold the stereotyped assumption that all clients must be unattractive or undesirable in some way, but I was sometimes amazed at the men who showed up at my door. Many of the attractive, vibrant guys who paid me did so because seeing a prostitute was easier (on the ego *and* the stopwatch) than going through the motions of cruising, courting, or risking sexual harassment charges at the office. Part of my attractiveness to men like this lies in the fact that arranging sex with me entails less negotiation and no bullshit—or, to put it very badly, because they know I'll say yes. In fact, I'll probably even initiate.

Boundaries—A professional will rarely decide to try to take over a client's life (though once in a while a client will get possessive about a whore). The boundary that distinguishes the commodified sex worker-client relationship (that is, the very fact that it's pay-for-play) gives both people space away from the usual assumptions that come with nonprofessional couplings. The client doesn't have to worry that I will call him at 3 a.m., try to undermine his marriage, or worse. This is the difference between me and, say, Monica Lewinsky, and to avoid his own personal Monicagate, many a man will gladly make a stop at the ATM.

This boundary also, I think, helps some clients feel comfortable enough to say what they want sexually. Part of that willingness, granted, is the fact that the client is paying for a service and that he understands the sex worker as someone to whom he can speak frankly. Bluntly, he is on the permissive side of the madonna/whore dichotomy. Once he's done, he can leave, and it's up to him whether he'll call back. If he's revealed himself too intimately, he never has to see the whore again. On the other hand, his intimate revelations may be *only* sexual: I know the erotic secrets of quite a number of men about whom I know virtually nothing else. I repeatedly saw one guy who liked to whimper, "Mommy! Mommy!" just before he came, but who never gave me a clue as to his profession and interests—things his *real* Mommy undoubtedly knew.

Partner Variety—Yes, I said it before: the majority of clients are married or otherwise partnered. This does not necessarily give them automatic access to sex, of course; even if it does, they may still want to do that thing the sociobiologists tell us all men want to do, namely, spread their seed far and wide. Never mind that their seed never leaves the reservoir tip of the condom—presumably that instinct is temporarily sated when a man fucks a new person, and for many men (related to Convenience), the best thing about the sex industry is that it offers a source of accessible new partners. My madams told me that some of their clients would see a new woman only once or twice, no matter how much they enjoyed her—and some of my clients said as much to me. This may be related to Boundaries, as well—there is less chance he'll form an intimate attachment with someone he only sees a time or two. It's a very common myth that no intimacy exists in a whore's exchange with her or his client, though some whores don't resist intimacy at all. On the other hand, some clients *do*—often, I think, to resist feeling adulterous. More than one brusque and businesslike client sported a white spot surrounded by tan on his ring finger—to a whore, a more obvious sign that the john is married than a wedding ring worn nonchalantly.

Perhaps with the same inner excitement that I felt as an adolescent when I began enumerating the sexual partners I had, certain clients seem interested in racking up numbers. For some, a new partner represents a new adventure even if he goes through exactly the same motions each time he has sex. Even my most loyal client, whom I saw for over nine years, has apparently seen just about every other whore in town. Come to think of it, he rarely saw me alone—he always called me for a double (that is, one client, two whores). He had perfected the art of maintaining a relationship even as he enjoyed variety.

Sexual Variety—I'm sure many people engage in essentially the same sexual practices over and over throughout their lives, but some like more variation, and the sex industry allows clients a place to easily negotiate for this. Many clients who want something that's not on the menu at home have learned to request it from a professional. It's often said that a whore has to do anything the client wants, which is ridiculous: except in situations of force or great need, prostitutes negotiate what they are/are not willing to do. (What we say we do may be contingent on the client: more than once I said, "I don't do anal," after a ham-handed hug of greeting convinced me that this guy would never get his clumsy mitts anywhere *near* my tender ass.)

Of course, most of us are probably willing (and know how) to do more than the amateurs. Additionally, many of us specialize in particular kinds of sex play, as can be readily seen when we advertise. (The most specialized sex worker of this type is the professional dominant, who may have fine-tuned her/his practice to an intense degree.)

Most important, plenty of clients have divergent sexual interests that are not welcome in their own bedrooms. They are into cross-dressing, S/M, anal play; they are bisexuals or fetishists; some erotic facet of their being is rejected by their partners (or they have never found the courage to bring it up at home). One of my long-term clients loved anal fisting, and everyone from his girlfriend to his therapist tried to talk him out of engaging in it. So he periodically called me in for an evening of friendly chat, warmed-up lube, and slow, deep penetration.

The sex industry often proves the safest container for what I think of as this everyday divergence, the great amount of sexual variety that bubbles under the surface of so-called "normal" life. I call it "everyday divergence" because these varying desires are so commonly seen by whores. Often completely outside of the communities that have developed to give support and space to people of diverse sexualities, throngs of men turn to whores with their secrets.

The Male Role—Being a client allows a man, on the one hand, to call the sexual shots, at least to the degree that he wants something the whore of the moment is prepared to deliver. In that sense, it facilitates him in living out the "Me Tarzan" fantasy—getting what he wants. But many clients experience the reality of the masculine role in another way: male sexuality is often unduly performance oriented, even mechanized. The man often has to make all the moves. With a whore, he can lie back and receive—something many men deeply appreciate, whether it takes the form of a blow job, a greased finger up the ass, or a full-on S/M scene.

Sexual Growth and Experimentation—Related to Sexual Variety, but, as I see it, a somewhat different phenomenon is the client who simply wants to be able to try new things. He may not incorporate each new type of play into his sexual repertoire, but he wants to play and explore. Sometimes he's bored with the old in-and-out; sometimes he sees the whore as a sexual expert who'll make a good guide to the unknown; sometimes he's a novelty queen. One of my clients (interestingly, a man who was very new to the sex industry) became jealous of my other clients and partners; when I reminded him that this was what I did for a living, he demanded that I trot him through all sorts of sexual variations, one after the other ("I might as well get what I'm paying for"). I fired him—he already *was* getting what he was paying for, and I don't need a bad attitude like that showing up every week.

Mostly, though, experimental clients were fun for me—I was in a period of intense sexual experimentation myself when I began working (in fact, whoring was part of that path for me), and I respected their desire to try something new. Sometimes this desire is triggered after a long period of "same old, same old": after years of near cookie-cutter sessions, one of my long-term clients decided he wanted to try getting fucked with a strap-on, and still later he wondered if I could find a guy to join us. Was his interest in sucking cock there all along, or did it emerge much later? I don't know—and, in fact, the john might not know, either.

Personal Comfort and Healing—This is an amorphous category that includes clients who mostly want to be touched (or who want to talk), middle-aged virgins, clients who want or who respond to sacred prostitutes, and johns who get no other source of sexual comfort or who have been wounded sexually. Working with these guys often feels like sex therapy or surrogacy; it is challenging and rewarding. My most profound experiences have been with this sort of client: the pedophile who hired me, an adult woman, to wear pigtails and engage him in a fantasy strong enough to blunt his desires for girls; the widower who wanted to be held when he talked about his late wife; the sweet, shy man with gynecomastia (enlarged breasts) and a terrible body image. The whore as healer or spiritual guide is an old archetype, from the sacred whore to the whore with the heart of gold, and clients who come to us openheartedly can, in many cases, evoke this archetype.

However, we and our clients come from the same culture, one that respects neither the whore nor the one who pays. It's true that whores bear the brunt of the legal system's attack (at least, we have until recently), but we all stand a good chance of coming from households in which sex was problematic, feared, disrespected, shrouded in silence, or abused. This exacerbates the need for sexual healing, but it also exacerbates erotophobia and whore hatred.

One way to metaphorically understand clients is as thirsty men who have found their way to a watering hole rumored by others to be poisoned. Their thirst wars with their fear: the decision to drink is often hard, but drink they do. This helps explain some of the negative attitudes and behaviors focused on whores, I believe: men are urged by the culture to a lower self-image by the act of paying for sex. Many don't buy into this, fortunately, but, of course, many do.

Some men see whores in lieu of masturbating; they believe so deeply that solo sex is shameful that the whore becomes a sort of human milking machine. Some men resent and fear anything that tempts them sexually—especially when they have to pay for it. Some men see whores to avoid intimacy. And a few men choose whores as the target of their own psychopathology, most likely rooted in abuse they themselves have received, wedded to a dangerous and volatile antipathy about sex.

Most men who see whores, though, at least *want* to like sex, and if they manage to come to terms with the implications of paying for it, there's a chance they can be socialized into decent clients, if not downright good ones. (Curious about what I consider a good client? It's not about dick size or even the size of his wallet. It's whether he's pleasant, respectful, clean, clear about what he wants, able to negotiate, and willing to have fun.)

In a perfect world, the sex industry would either vanish, replaced by a system that treats sex like a pleasant, natural good available to (and enjoyed by) everyone, or it would thrive aboveground, equitably, safely, fully accessible to women as well as men. No, I'm not holding my breath. But to get there we'll have to stop demonizing johns for wanting to get their rocks off, and to do *that,* we'll have to stop generalizing about and stereotyping them. Men *don't* want one thing—in my experience, they want a real variety of sensations and experiences, some of which defy simplistic notions about male sexuality. If we can urge the culture to rein in its judgments, maybe we can get a little more support from johns in our own fight for respect.

−15−

In Love with My Work

Scott O'Hara

When I showed up at the hotel room door of my first official trick, I was terrified. Not of him, per se, or of having sex for money, and certainly not of getting AIDS (this was 1985, I think; I probably already had AIDS, but just didn't know it yet); quite simply, I was terrified that he might be a vice cop. I still don't know how realistic this fear was. All the hustlers I've talked to downplay the danger, at least in San Francisco, but I think most of them don't share my special antipathy of the police. Just seeing a cop makes me burn with anger, and I'm seriously afraid that being arrested by one of those scumbags might make me do something foolish, like try to kill the fucker. And I really don't want to spend the rest of my life in prison.

As a sex professional, I was, frankly, quite an amateur. I never took a job that I didn't want to take; I never felt coerced into sex "for the money." I had all the money I needed to live modestly; when I started making films, I did so because I loved doing it. And when I put an ad in *The Advocate* classifieds (the one and only such ad I ever placed), it was because I was eager to discover what the world of hustling was like. Terrified, yes, but very curious.

I didn't answer many calls. That is, I got a lot of phone calls, but most of them were jack-off callers, late at night. Not very entertaining. I only made dates with three tricks—which was just about enough to pay for the ad. All of them were out-of-towners; all of them were perfectly nice men. But I discovered that sex isn't really very much fun when you're vibrating with tension, wondering whether he's gonna pick up his badge at any minute and flash it at you. Ruins the sex. At least, it did for me. I couldn't just relax and enjoy it. So I stopped running the ad. I kept getting occasional late-night phone calls, though, for the next six months.

It was the live performances and the films that I found much more satisfying. At the time, I'd never heard of a performer being arrested for prostitution (I think it's been tried once since then in Los Angeles, but I don't know the outcome of the case), so I felt pretty safe. And as I told people, repeatedly, when I trick with a client, I'm satisfying one man (well, two—presumably). When I'm onstage, I can watch dozens of men jerking off over me; I can see the lust in their eyes, the need in their gonads. But when I make a video, I'm satisfying thousands of men, possibly millions in the decades to come. That's worth something to me. I'm happy to be able to report that, ten years later, it's still true: men are still watching many of my videos, they're still jerking off to them, they're still telling me about their favorite parts (and critiquing some of their less-favored parts). And I still get an incredible charge out of knowing those facts. Not many men get the chance to give pleasure to as many people as I have; that's a better payment than any paycheck.

When I worked at the Campus Theatre, sometimes an audience member would hang around afterward and offer me money to have sex. I'd usually brush him off, but more than once, when I found him attractive, I would say, "No, I won't have sex with you for money, but I'll do it for free." A couple of them took me up on it; a couple others turned me down, to my surprise. And it took me a while, but I finally realized that my response was turning them off. These guys wanted validation for their economic choices, as much as for their appearance. When I told them that I didn't want their money, the subliminal message was that sex with me wasn't worth paying for, that they were stupid for offering.

The next time I got such an offer (it happened to be from a regular customer, whom I'd seen in the front row jacking off on a number of occasions), I just said yes. He told me that all he wanted was, literally, a private show. Usually that's a euphemism for sex, but he just wanted me to jack off for him, in his living room, in front of his mirrored wall. And I did, gladly. It was a fine show—I took along my boom box and performance tape and did my show exactly as I usually did it onstage—but I have to admit that the drive back into the city afterward was a bit uncomfortable. Still, I got the impression that I gave him exactly what he wanted, and like I say, that's a satisfying sensation.

What did he pay me? I haven't the foggiest idea. I probably asked him for the same fee I was getting from the Campus at that point. Getting paid for it didn't mean much to me, frankly, but paying for it obviously meant a lot to him. It meant that I was an item of value, something to be remembered and cherished. I probably should have asked more (and I wonder, today, if he had a camera hidden behind the mirrored wall).

Money has always had a secondary place in my life. Money is only a means to an end; being wealthy allows you the privilege of not worrying about the mundane, day-to-day problems that poor people have to deal with, but it doesn't guarantee you any form of actual happiness. Would it have been different if I'd been raised in poverty, or if I'd run away and hit the streets, hustling at age fifteen after spending the summer in France? The morning I was catching the plane home, at the end of that summer, I seriously contemplated the option of missing the plane, just losing myself on the streets of Paris, selling my body. I liked the idea, and I knew I could do it. I was an adolescent queer boy in search of all the sex I could find— but it scared me too. Hell, I'd only lost my virginity three months before! I took the safe way out. Most people think I made the right choice. I sometimes wonder.

The thing about money that most people seem to miss is that it only does you any good if you use it. When men use it to buy sex, that's a valid expression of their values. When they use it to buy a house, or car, or a gourmet meal, ditto. When it's put in a savings account, ditto. But too many of the men who are working their asses off—and I'm talking about corporate work here, not street work— don't seem to see it as a means to an end. "If I make enough money, then I'll be happy" is pure insanity—about as successful a strategy as, "If I have enough sex, then I'll be sated." Neither commodity is evil, but neither works like a gas tank. You can't "fill up." The delightful aspect of prostitution is that it allows those people who have an excess of one commodity to exchange it for the one that they're lacking. That's what the free market is all about.

That pretty much sums up my attitude toward work of any sort. If you're doing it just for the money, you're in the wrong field. Oh, sure, everyone needs money to eat. But there are enough occupations in this world, people get paid for enough bizarre types of stuff, that everyone should be able to find a job that actually gives him or her pleasure, as well as paying the bills (some places, I'm told, people even get paid for writing!). In my ideal world, I have to say, sex work as a full-time profession would not be an option for most people, simply because there would be so many part-timers doing "freelance." Oh, I'm sure there would still be openings for those with special talents. With my ability to suck my own dick, I probably would still be a curiosity, and people would pay to watch me do it—but if prostitution were destigmatized, I think your average housewife or construction worker would probably want to try it out on the weekends.

As the supply increased, the demand would decrease, until a balance would be reached. So, from a prostitute's point of view, thank God for prohibition! It's what pays the bills for many a marginal hustler: the ones who, from a rational perspective, don't have anything special in the sexual marketplace. What they're selling isn't, strictly speaking, their bodies, but their willingness to flout convention, to risk arrest and social opprobrium, and the potential subsequent reduction of their value in other job markets.

What caused me to go out in search of money in exchange for sex? Was I an emotionally starved child, in need of ego strokes and attention? Maybe. Yawn. I don't care what psychological motivations you want to ascribe to my performances; I was onstage, being admired and envied and jerked off over by dozens of men nightly. Money can't buy that. Oh, maybe Bill Gates, with all his billions, could hire an auditorium full of men to worship him nightly, but I doubt that it would be the same. What made it special for me was the knowledge that these men were actually paying good money to watch me (and to top it off, they were giving me a show that I'd been known to pay money to see at various jack-off clubs around town!). That demonstrated to me just how they really felt about me; the pocketbook doesn't lie. They weren't doing it because I was buying them dinner. Money for sex is a very honest relationship: no one's trying to mislead anyone else. And that, in my book, makes it pretty special. Honesty is a rare enough commodity; combine it with pleasure, and I think you've got a working definition of love.

TRICKS AND TREATS

−16−

Thirty Years

Coffee

I used to work at a massage parlor right outside of the gate to Fort Lee Army Base. With most tricks there, it wasn't a physical thing; it was just something kinky. Like the guy who took his golf stick and putted eggs at a girl's cunt, or the guy that liked to suck your thumb while you waved bye-bye. There was a woman trick who used to like boiled sweet potatoes thrown between her legs. You had to cook the sweet potatoes until they were very, very soft, then you'd just throw them and watch them splurt.

I guess most of the tricks down South came to us because they couldn't get what they wanted at home; most of them were married. We had a group of girls who'd try to get into the guys' homes because we were bisexual, so we liked women too; we liked orgies and all that stuff. We'd try and get the tricks' wives involved, and when we succeeded, the wives were usually more generous than the husbands.

We had a whole lot of weird tricks. There's this whore story we used to tell one another. There was a man who'd had sex every way that you can possibly imagine, so he had a contract out that if any girl could show him a new way to have sex, he would give that girl a thousand dollars. There was no way this man had not had sex. He'd had anal sex, he'd had sex with men, he'd had sex with multiple partners, sex in public, sex with animals, sex with corpses, sex with snakes. He'd seen and done everything. This one woman came and said, "I know something that you've never done before. I don't even have to take my clothes off to do it." He asked, "What is it?" She said, "You got my money?" He said, "You haven't even

121

taken off your clothes." She said, "I don't have to take off my clothes." This girl had a glass eye, and she opened the socket of her eye and said screw me in my eyeball. So he had to give her the thousand. Plus tip.

We had this one person who wanted to spit on your face. I always thought it was okay because at least I didn't have to have sex, but he'd spit on you as much as he wanted, until you'd get to the point where if he spit on you one more time, you were going to whoop his ass. He'd just want to sit and talk to you and all of the sudden he'd spit in your face. He wouldn't warn you.

Then there was the guy in New York we called Dracula. He was this rich man who got his limousine to come and pick you up; the driver took you out to this mansion, and the butler opened the door. You'd go in and see candles lit everywhere, and if you looked hard enough, you'd see a huge casket. He got his thing off by hearing you scream after he raised up the casket. He would be inside, and the louder you screamed or the more scared you looked, the bigger the tip you'd get.

I used to live with this gay man. I loved gay men because they taught me how to be a woman: I had eight brothers and no sisters, so it took a gay man to show me how to act. This gay guy had a boyfriend who was a top, and we wanted to change him and make him a bottom; he said, "Since my man wants to screw you, I'm going to let him get what he wants." His boyfriend got all excited because I was like a special thing in the house. He got on top of me and started going at it and his boyfriend got on top of him. Then he started screaming, we all began to fight, and the gay guy hit him on the head with a hammer. Thinking that he was dead, we took him and wrapped him up in a sheet, put him in the car, took him to the park, and since it was fall, we put him in a ditch and covered him up with leaves. Then we went to a bootlegger's bar and got drunk. When we got home, he was sitting up in the living room—we thought we had killed him, and he had beat us back home. Then we started to fight all over again.

I worked for thirty years down South, everywhere you can imagine, and up here in New York, on the streets and in parlors. It got violent a lot of the time. Many times, I got close to getting killed, but I never got cut up—no body parts cut off of me. I was one of the lucky ones. I could always find a way to talk the guy out of it or sex him out of it. I'd been raped so many times, I figured if I just started to help them, that would discourage them: they need that fear in you.

Then there were a few men I call mechanics; they can make you do things you didn't know your body could do. I met one or two of those guys in thirty years. I'd let them have their way for free, just so they'd come back to me.

A lot of prostitutes are tricks themselves: they need to pay some-one to do what they want, exactly the way they want it, to get them off. Today, if I see someone I really want, I'm a trick. I'll pay them, but if I can't get what I want, I don't bother them anymore. Just like a trick.

I used to work on army bases as a stripper at NCO clubs. This girl who was 4'5" was my first female lover. I used to take her to dance and stuff. Then I'd get these big parties, all these GIs in a ware-house, or some place like an armory. They'd want me to get four girls: I took my girlfriend because we wanted to make most of the money.

In each corner of the warehouse, they had a military ambulance, and every time a guy would finish with a girl in the ambulance, he'd sound the siren. I used to be an acid freak back then; I used to stay totally blind off that stuff. They had a huge bowl of potato salad. I put my little girlfriend in this bowl and made a snowman on her with the potato salad. We were dancing, and it was amazing how I incorporated putting her in this potato salad and then taking pitchers of beer and pouring it all over us, and then I walked across the table and started feeding the GIs off our bodies, and they were eating it.

I used to get paid to go to orgies. The men all called themselves straight, so it was hard to get them to mingle and get them in the positions that I wanted them in. They were too afraid they might touch one another. That was the part of the orgies that used to really cream me—getting the men into compromising positions. I'd say, "I want to suck both of your dicks at the same time," so that they would bump their dick heads together. I knew they were homopho-bic. They thought I was just doing my job, but I was playing a game with them. There was a method to my madness: it wasn't just about getting money; it was about what I could get people to do.

A Few Friends

Faye Rowland

I had reached a point in my life where my only means of support was selling my transitorily unique body. I was determined to stay off the streets and had everything necessary for in-call/out-call work. I had studied the varied genres of back-page ads in the smut tabloids, so composing a likely one wasn't taxing: "Gorgeous She-male at your service. Call . . ."

Las Vegas After Dark was the leading smut publication in town, so I went to their office to take out an ad. "Six weeks minimum," I was told. That was one hundred and fifty dollars. Somewhat dubiously, I paid it. "Dubious," as I was afraid I'd end up paying more for the ad than what I'd make from it. I needn't have worried.

The ad appeared a couple days later. I can almost pinpoint the exact minute. At that moment, the phone started ringing and only stopped when I unplugged it. My entry into the sex profession hadn't been thought out beyond placing the ad. I answered the first call with a hesitant "Hello . . ."

My first client was a nice local man and a connoisseur of she-males. He recognized fresh meat in my ad and hastened to respond. I gave him directions and told him to hurry on over, then rushed about trying to get myself sexy. This was rather hectic since, as I've said, the phone wouldn't stop ringing. While getting ready, I booked five more clients, timing them at forty-five minutes each. Finally, in confusion, I unplugged the phone.

The doorbell rang. That "nice connoisseur" was certainly more professional than I was during my "initiation." He seemed oddly detached from my jittery clumsiness, required only head—and he took just fifteen minutes. On leaving, he kindly pressed fifty dollars upon me. I had been too distraught to even think about prices. As he went out the door, he casually alluded to being a police officer. I stood there at the door, transfixed by a medley of shock waves reverberating within me. This thing actually worked—I had made money; I hadn't been murdered or arrested or whatever else—and this guy was a cop, or so he said. In the months to come, I'd have less and less reason to doubt him, as I was to become the unofficial mascot of the Las Vegas Metropolitan Police Department (with emphasis on the K-9 unit).

My first client was barely out of sight when my next client came wandering into the courtyard of my apartment complex. I could already see that I'd have to space these guys out farther so they wouldn't stack up. I lived on the second floor, which helped a bit, and the highly transient population of my apartment complex also helped. But still, one doesn't want to be too obvious.

The hundreds of clients that I was to encounter over the next year and a half are mostly just blurs brushing against my memory, but there are some I vividly recall. A few of these, I wish had tarried. As a neophyte to sex work, what astounded me most about the clientele was their banal "normalcy." Being a transgendered prostitute, just starting out in the only business where transgendered people are welcome, I had no idea what to expect. What kind of men prefer, or are at least curious about, transsexuals? It was a pleasant surprise to find the majority of them quite gentlemanly and even urbane.

The Western man's "man" is narrowly positioned toward the macho pole of sexuality's continuum. If the otherwise manly man wishes, perhaps, to experience passive anal intercourse, a female prostitute will be somewhat limited in the task; a male prostitute will rather too directly confront the client with his own sexual ambivalence. The transsexual prostitute fills these niches just so. In any event, the dude sure the hell isn't going to ask his wife to strap on a dildo and butt-fuck him.

Probably half the clients I saw fit this analysis. The things that these men brought me never impressed me as being particularly eye-opening, hardly worthy of terms such as "disgusting" or "perverse." Personally, I am at a loss as to what may have been the most disgusting thing I was ever called upon to do—high-end disgust-

ing—not the scaled-down hijinks that would offend Ma and Pa
Lunchpail, the Pope, or even the Dalai Lama, but just that sort of
thing that a "Divine" or a Warhol or maybe a Mapplethorpe
could've found momentarily amusing.

Jim, who became one of my regulars, was close to sixty and had
retired relatively young, but the expense associated with a cata-
strophic illness brought him back to the job market. His illness had
left him with a catheter valve in his stomach, but he usually didn't
wear his colostomy bag when he came over. His glass eye was a
souvenir from some other accident. Jim was nice and easy, and all
he ever wanted was a blow job. I had experimented on him at first,
rimming both his eye socket and the colostomic opening. While
blowing him, I'd penetrate his urethral with the cap of a pen, which
I had sucked tight against the tip of my tongue. I'd plunge the cap
softly and slowly into his urethra canal. Jim was never keen on such
pleasures and only wanted basic head. As I said, nice and easy.

More of a chore was Donny. He was a big baby and demanded all
the attention to which babies are heir. Over some months, he had
assembled a considerable cache of supplies and equipment at my
apartment: dozens of his cotton diapers (big babies hate the dispos-
able ones), nursing bottles, baby oil and powder, bright blue booties
(size *very* large), and anything else Donny fancied to be babyish. A
typical session with Donny would run about two hours and be
worth upward of two hundred dollars. He would show up with a
diaper on already under his trousers and would soil himself as soon
as he came through the door. Then it would be my task to undress
him as he flayed and flopped about, cooing and ahhing, and generally acting like, well, a baby. After I stripped him, I'd have to lead
him to the bath and clean him up. After drying him, I'd powder and
strategically oil him, then pin his oversized diaper into place. Then
it would be time for Donny's breast-feeding.

At the time, I had been on hormones for a year and a half, and
was just developing into a B cup. I'd sit on the floor, bracing my
back against the wall, whereupon Donny would sprawl his two
hundred-plus pounds directly onto my chest. Donny would take one
of my nipples into his mouth and commence sucking. I wasn't
making milk (yet), so I'd allow a trickle from a glass of warm milk
to dribble onto my breast, where it drained down to my nipple and

into Donny's sucking mouth. I always felt supremely ridiculous during these "feedings," but for the money Donny paid, I was always able to keep my mouth shut.

After the feeding, I'd again lead Donny by the hand to my bedroom and put him to "sleep." Naturally, several lullabies would be in order. On other occasions, Donny'd want to be seated at my table, bib in place, while I spooned him some Gerbers. Other times, he'd want to be spanked for some naughty thing he'd contrived to do. Donny was one of my best clients, and long after I had quit the business, his nursing bottles came in handy when I had to wean a litter of stray puppies I'd found.

A less pliant customer was Bob. Less pliant and a tad scary—and more than a tad cheap. Even so, Bob gave me some of my wildest and most exciting trade.

Bob liked things rough and public. My first session with him was at my apartment. Thereafter, he'd arrange to meet me at a motel on the southern reaches of the strip. The motel, since demolished, had been upscale in its time. By this point, it served as a lagoon for the tidal surges of transient populations, the milieu being bikers, street prostitutes, displaced ex-blue-collar families living on wit and will, and the subturf of the drug scene—the also-rans of the mostly white-trash world. Just the place, perhaps, where a transsexual wouldn't be deemed particularly remarkable. And no one, as a rule, ever called the cops. Which was just as well.

After Bob had me strip naked, leaving only hose and pumps on, he would tie me facedown on an old formica table in the motel kitchenette. He'd then take an hour alternately whipping my ass with a lamp cord and butt-fucking me. He whipped pretty hard, but seemed to know the point beyond which not to go. Being prone and spread-eagled on the table, and still having (at the time) a penis, I'd writhe about, straining at the cords binding my wrists and ankles and heaving my weight about on my prick. Bob would be aware of my self-stimulation, and as my excitement grew, he would renew the lashing with vigor. As long as he limited the lashing to my ass and upper legs, the pleasure of masturbation and the thrill of the whipping outweighed the discomfort. Somewhere around this point, Bob would penetrate me. A climax, at least for me, would occur shortly thereafter. This climax was, however, a prelude . . .

After Bob withdrew his dick from my ass, he would drag the whole table, with me still gasping on it, over to the door. He would position the table and throw open the door so that anyone passing down the hall would get a load of my gaping, steaming, lubricated ass. Bob's idea was to offer me up to anyone who came along. I don't know if I was ready to go that far—and I didn't. Though plenty of men would pass by and stay to watch, none of them felt bold enough to enjoy the bounty. I think Bob was indulging in a bit of vicarious public humiliation. As for me, the sheer wanton thrill of being bound and compromised on public display was sometimes enough to make me come.

If it was late enough, and if the pool of potential witnesses seemed mellow enough, I'd let Bob fuck me right there in that doorway, exposed to the whole inner courtyard and its denizens. Needless to say, Bob had to pay me handsomely for my services, and I suppose his willingness to pay fostered in my mind the belief that I was in control; recalling those scenes, I really don't know. And, during our "shows," I often wondered how many waste cases got their rocks off on Bob's dime. As nasty as one can be isn't all that nasty after all, if a little soap and water suffice to clean one up. The nastiest thing I was ever called to do, I refused.

This guy called in the afternoon; he was younger than me. He wanted an in-call session. I gave him directions. When he arrived, I saw that his youthful voice hadn't misled me—he was *very* good-looking. He was nervous, despite apparently having promised himself not to be. I sat him down and kept a conversation going so as to draw out the nervousness before setting about business.

I proffered the inevitable, "Are you visiting Vegas?" He admitted so and added that he was there for his wedding. I kept a straight face and asked him, "When?" "Tomorrow," he answered. I stifled my revulsion. Suddenly, I just had to know what kind of person he was.

"Uh, don't you think it's a little odd to seek the services of a hooker just before you get married—particularly a specialist, like me?" He seemed a little embarrassed by the question, but not defensive.

"Well, yeah, maybe," he replied. This was well before the Hugh Grant affair, which might have given me another perspective. At the time, I found it hard to conceal the loathing I was feeling for this guy. I had determined that he'd be leaving shortly, unfulfilled.

And that's how it played out. But, that this handsome and bright young man, supposedly in the thrall of prenuptial love, should christen his marriage with betrayal loomed in my mind as a palpable presence—like some atavistic, archetypal dinosaur: predatory— a feeder on human faith. To this day, I haven't been able to clean off the creeps that guy gave me.

Just as numerous as the clients who see the transsexual prostitute as an uncritical surrogate are those who are decidedly turned on by the shemale. Of these, it seems to me there are two types: one who sees the transsexual as a neutral vessel, that is, the "third sex," suitable for exotic experiments; and my favorite type, the "tranny chaser."

Thad was a prime example of the first type. All Thad wanted to do was give head, but not to a man. To use his own words, he wanted "pretty with dick." He'd come over and go down on me for hours on end. Naturally, I didn't mind these sessions at all, and I'd go real easy on the price just to keep him committed. I'd seat my weight against the edge of a high-backed chair, hitch up my skirt, and spread my legs wide. Thad would set to work between the garters. He wanted me whored up to the max so I'd go crazy with the pleasure he would give me; I'd get a little tipsy on wine and do poppers and sit there chain-smoking—which rendered me pretty much as desired. Being on hormones, there wouldn't be much, if any, semen when I came, which always seemed to disappoint Thad. Eventually, Thad wandered away in search of lusher founts.

"Monica" was, in "her" way, the same type as Thad. "She" wasn't a transsexual, or even a transvestite, just an unassuming man who needed, from time to time, to get in touch with his inner slut. Monica would come over and we'd play dress-up—and since she would wear my clothes, and had a tendency to stretch them out of shape, I had to charge her a heavy premium, which she was quite willing to pay. But Monica wanted me to fuck her as well, which I was, by then, unable to do. Monica also wandered away, in search of, uh, harder founts. It's always astonished me how many people feel that a transsexual is just the person to go to when they want to get fucked.

Then there are the tranny chasers, my favorites. Tranny chasers are those men who seem to naturally appreciate the transsexual for the woman she is or is becoming. Tranny chasers are pretty much willing to accept the transsexual on her own terms, without imposing their own fantasies upon her—as she herself *is* the fantasy. It's been my experience that a great many guys become tranny chasers following an unknowing involvement with a transsexual—making their discovery later on and, with reflection, finding that they liked it. They can't explain it any more than the transsexual can—the most mystical allure of the transgendered person does, it seems, appear to be somewhat archetypal.

One problem for me with the tranny chaser was the prospect of romance. I'm always a sucker, always ready to blow off my fees and renounce my wayward life, for the right guy. Like Jean. Jean was Cajun and worked for a major trucking company. His route led him through Las Vegas, and he gave me a call. "Come on over," I told him, and he did. He parked his truck in the minimall parking lot across the street from my apartment. He was between loads and was bound for LA to pick up his next trailer, so he warned me that he "couldn't stay all night." I suppressed a laugh, not knowing what he knew, and said that was "too bad."

We talked for a long while, and I found him to be increasingly fascinating, with his Cajun accent and French phrases. We finally retired to my bedroom and made hard love—and I discovered his secret: eight-plus inches. Afterward, he commented that time was running short, but he wanted to take me out to dinner before he left, and that was it—I had experimented with everything the Kama Sutra and my imagination had suggested, but it didn't take too long for me to realize that men just flat-out refuse to see sex as a path to "enlightenment," or anything else, save lightening their load. So when their only thought is *not* to split with all haste, you know they actually like you—and I certainly was falling into "like" with the big hairy bear.

We went to dinner in Jean's truck cab. Riding around in a big-rig cab is a singular experience. One is several times higher off the ground than normally when driving, and one can see straight down into everyone else's cars. The voyeuristic urge comes on strong, and the other drivers don't disappoint. After Jean and I ate dinner, we agreed that he'd drop by again in three days on his turnaround run. I had forgotten all about my fee.

Jean and I also agreed that when he returned, I'd accompany him on his run toward the East Coast, which required that I register as a partner/passenger with his company—which, in turn, meant that I would finally have to get my driver's license changed to reflect my appropriate name. To expedite the process, as well as for the friendlier attitudes, I drove to Barstow in California and visited the DMV there. Jean had supplied me with the address of a friend in Lancaster that I could use as my own in obtaining a California license. I returned to Las Vegas with a temporary permit that had my proper name on it—which I photocopied. On the copy, I artfully changed the "M" to "F," then copied the altered copy, and gave it to Jean when he returned. He faxed the new copy to his company. We were all set and took off for Denver.

We wound our way slowly through the Rocky Mountains, surmounting grade after grade, snaking around the winds and coils, and commenting on the wisdom of having truck ramps as we barreled down the descending grades. A cooling stop of fifteen to twenty minutes was necessary at the top of each grade. Jean would make his brake checks; then we would retire to the sleeping cabin behind the front seats and get in one more fuck before the next grade.

The sleeping cabin was as sumptuously appointed as it was possible for two hundred cubic feet to be. It reminded me of a space capsule for decidedly decadent astronauts. Despite what many people believe, it is possible to take it up the ass while supine, and I'd arch my neck back and distractedly gaze through the porthole window, inches from my face, as Jean pounded away. Sometimes I'd see an eagle or a hawk gliding overhead—sometimes the face of some other trucker pressed up against the glass, looking for the rig's driver. At a truck stop near Grand Junction, Jean bought an "If it's rockin', don't bother knockin'" sign, which shepherded our privacy the rest of the way to Denver. (Those signs seem to work in reverse though.)

We rolled down the last grade and entered Denver's suburbs. In town, Jean dropped off the trailer and picked up another. We had one day to get back over the Rockies and into Salt Lake City. Plenty of time, Jean insisted, for him to show me Denver. When I asked him how we'd get around on the grand tour, he just winked. His plan was to drop his load and get around in the truck cab. Which is what we did.

Jean figured we'd pick up the trailer and get on the highway around two a.m. the next morning, which gave us five hours or so for serious partying—but dropping the load gave me misgivings, and when I found out that doing so was a major violation of company policy, I was really worried. But Jean just laughed it off, saying he'd done it "a million times."

Jean had a predilection for country-western joints—which only heightened my qualms. But he knew half the people in the places where we went, and I guess he wanted to show me off. The women in those bars were few and uninspiring, and I received no end of attention, which of course I found very pleasant, but still . . .

My attempts to limit Jean's alcohol intake were meeting with little success, and eventually, the inevitable happened—Jean got into a fight. Some other drunk made fun of Jean's Cajun accent, and after a round of insults and challenges, they lit into each other. The contending parties were hustled outside, where the stupidity continued. I knew the cops had been called, and I did my best to get away with Jean, but, as I was learning, he was rather too much the "normal" man—congenitally incapable of listening to reason. The cops duly arrived, but even then it wouldn't have been too late to leave. But sure enough, Jean talked himself into getting arrested.

Jean was locked up overnight, and that was more than long enough for the company to be informed, and to fire him for dropping his load. They sent over a local contract driver to collect the rig.

I saw Jean once more in Denver, after he was let out of jail. He wanted me to stay on with him, said he'd "get something going." But his stupidity outweighed his attractions, and I took the "dog" back to Vegas that afternoon. Though I never saw Jean again, I had to screw around with the legacy he left me—trying to get hold of my new driver's license. It took several letters and a lot of phone calls, but Jean's friend finally forwarded it to me.

One of my favorite tranny chasers wasn't even a client. A cop, yes; a client, no. I was out for a stroll on the Strip, pretty close to the "Sahara," on a persistently sultry October evening. I wasn't "working," though it probably seemed so to a casual observer. I was wearing a black, skintight body suit, with lots of silver accessories and big hair-sprayed hair. I saw the police vehicle as I approached, about half a block ahead. I surreptitiously crossed the street, so as not to get too close. Not surreptitiously enough. As I passed the cop, he called me over.

I recrossed the street and approached. The cop was sitting in a four-wheel-drive scout type of vehicle, all nicely painted up in black and white, with red and blue lights, antennas, speakers, and almost "cow catcher" bumpers. He was positioned there, in "reserve," waiting until called as backup for whatever trouble flared up on the Strip. I came up to the driver's side, and he said, through the open window, "You're going to get in trouble."

"I'm not doing anything wrong," I sniffed, and my pouting wasn't affected. I was already becoming incensed at what I imagined would be a hassling, or worse. The cop grinned and repeated, "You're still going to get in trouble."

"I'm not 'working'—I'm not a hooker," I managed to say, which wasn't a complete lie, as I wasn't working the streets, and what I did in privacy didn't concern street cops.

"Come here," the cop urged. I stepped right up to the window and looked at his face. Through my rising irritation, I couldn't help noticing that he was young and good-looking. "I'm really not doing anything wrong," I said calmly. The cop looked me up and down.

"Get in," he ordered. As I walked around the front of the big vehicle to the passenger side, I saw the cop stretch across the seats and unlock the door. I climbed in. I noticed the lettering on the hood as I passed: "K-9 Unit."

The cop's eyes were fair and bright, and his expression, not quite a grin, was like he was doing his best to keep from smiling at me. He kept his eyes on me and said, "When you go out like that— you're going to get into trouble." I was still sure that I was going to be arrested and was trying to control my anger.

"I've got a right to dress any way I want—there's lots of women out here dressed up way more than me, and they ain't doing anything wrong either."

"What are you so nervous about?" he asked, now openly smiling.

"I'm not nervous—I'm afraid." Using the word "afraid" seemed to hit the right note. There had been a police incident a few weeks earlier: off-duty plainclothes cops had kicked in a man's door and killed him, all without a warrant, probable cause, or anything else. Ironically, this man's name had been Charles King—the Rodney King beating would occur in just a few more weeks.

"It's okay; you don't have to worry about anything." The cop was still smiling and now openly amused. Just then, something very cold and very wet pressed itself firmly into the nape of my neck. I shrieked and lunged forward, catching myself up against the dashboard and knocking both a flashlight and a radio handset off the dash and onto the floor.

As the handset yo-yoed up and down on its coil, I snapped around to see what had goosed my neck. Through the wide gauge metal grill that backed the seats protruded the snout of what appeared to be a wolf, whose moist sienna eyes calmly regarded me through the mesh. I became aware of the cop chuckling, and as he caught and reseated the dangling handset, he addressed his dog, "Now, Pring, don't be rude." The gigantic German shepherd thumped its tail.

"Pring?" I asked.

"Yeah, we call him that because he likes potato chips. Technically, his name is Prince, so it's close enough so as not to confuse him." Hearing himself being discussed, the dog's tail thumped again. "Where are you going?" the cop asked.

"To, um, I'm just walking around checking out the sights."

"You live in Vegas?"

"Uh huh." Prince was nuzzling my neck again, and this time I found it relaxing. They double-teamed me: Prince working on my neck, his partner engaging me in light conversation. It slowly dawned on me that he was hitting on me. "What's your name?" I asked.

"David," he said slowly. "Yours?"

"Faye." I suddenly felt shy. My indignation had disappeared. We talked for a while and listened to the periodic blasts of static and chatter that issued loudly from the radio. Occasionally, David would pick up and curtly answer one of the blasts.

Prince had lain down and was relaxed, though alert. Pedestrians moving up and down the strip near us would see the police vehicle and pass with a degree of circumspection, until they noticed the dog, at which they would venture a longer look, even at the risk of making eye contact with the cop.

One of the passersby was a good-looking woman who had seen better times. She was dressed just as provocatively as I. She gave us a quick glance and turned away, raising her nose in apparent disdain. "Now there's a pair of cold witch's tits," Dave drolled.

"As cold as a cop's dick?" I answered, just a little too fast for thought.

David regarded me with a pensive stare. "Out," he said.

David leaned across the seats and opened the door for me. I shrugged and clambered out. He snapped the door shut. I walked away, going about twenty feet, when the police scout roared out of its parking space and tore off down the Strip. Prince kept his eyes on me as the car sped off. I'd sit in the scout with Dave and Prince again, though it wouldn't be for several weeks.

My affair with Dave would proceed unevenly over the next year and would even, surprisingly, survive the startling denouement that always comes with us trannies. One of the side effects of the affair was my abandonment of the "business." I paid for my operation with the savings from my "career." As I look back on my experiences, I see them as the swan song of my youth.

–18–

Scrapbook

D-L Alvarez

Manuel and Rudy

First, he's a chemical ghost with fuzzy holes for eyes. Then color bleeds into his face and into the background. His pupils blossom into two gold-specked irises burned with the white scar of the camera's flash. This Polaroid of Manuel tells a story of five minutes ago. In it, he washes his hands, wearing a T-shirt Rudy gave him and, though you can't see it in this photo, the chain I gave him under that. His own shirt was soiled with blood and shit—Rudy had a little accident. In the picture, he winks at the camera, winks at me. His wink says, *Hey, something disgusting just happened, but we can deal, us guys. Guys like us, we get by.*

Rudy isn't in this picture. He's in the living room mopping up. He set to work on that floor before he even bothered to clean himself, but the mess that he is, like color in a Polaroid, can't be contained. It spreads into the room the way a bruise gathers courage under the skin: slowly, starting with the most basic outline, a ghost of violence. Later, given a little time, details push forward and puff up the surface with the dark ugly history of recent events. Rudy does this to the room, crowds it with evidence of himself, until Manuel and I have to leave.

"Good-bye, Rudy." I gather my stuff and hold open the door for Manuel. Rudy leans his fat on the mop. His big eyes try desperately to gather something that might appeal to us; they flash question marks that are really just lies.

Grandma and Victor

Trapped in the vise of my legs, Grandma's fleshy visage is pinched in a tight bouquet of folds gathered round doll lips that go,

"Ooooo, uh, ooooo." I'm not that strong, but my opponent is a pushover. His real name is Norm (or is it Noam?), but he likes it when I say, "Had enough, Grandma?" The scissors hold allows me an opportunity to thrust my pelvis forward and rub the crotch of the bikini briefs he bought for this occasion against his chin. Like everything in this apartment, the underwear is blue, baby blue with midnight blue tiger stripes. The exception would be Grandma and me, though he comes close, with skin so pale it's blue in sheen, until I crush parts of it: his face and, with hands behind my back, his nipples, turning them bright pink while he jerks off. His safe word, which he's never had to use, is another term of relation, "Uncle." Unless I'm strangling him—something else he likes—then he should flash a peace sign if I go too far. On this occasion, I wind up sitting on most of his face, his eyes peeking up from behind my balls, which have slipped out of the tight undies. When he comes, a dollop hits me on the small of the back. He wipes it off with a scented blue Kleenex that sits in a blue crocheted Kleenex box cover at the bedside. Then we sit in this aquarium and leaf through one scrapbook pasted with photos of wrestlers and a second full of the "escorts" (his word) he used to see.

The nickname, Grandma, was given to him by one of his favorites. Turning a page, he says, "This is Victor in front of the Picasso in Chicago." The boy in the photo is in his early twenties. An open shirt shows two silver chains against a dark hairless chest. Grandma saved up from his job to take Victor on this vacation. Together they visited four-star restaurants and wrestled in budget hotels.

Another picture of Victor in suit and tie, his dark hair is greased back and he raises his wine glass to the camera. "You're not supposed to take photos in restaurants like that, but he was so excited. 'C'mon Grandma,' he kept saying, 'get one with Chicago in the background.' The flash obscures the skyline, tsk, but it's a good picture of Victor."

E. T.

So as not to ruffle security at the Hilton, I wear an overcoat to hide the police uniform underneath. Mr. Thorton, in room 312A, comes to town four times a year on business. He designs lighting for the exteriors of large buildings. He likes to be slapped across the face, then spat on. I find, whatever else I'm doing to Mr. Thorton, Ed Thorton, or "loser," as he likes to be referred to, if he ever starts to space out, a simple slap or spit wad brings him back quick. He also likes watersports, fisting, greyhounds (the mixed drink of vodka and grapefruit juice), and the films of W. C. Fields. (Once, after a session, he invited me to hang out and watch the comedian on one of the cable channels. I have to admit, I'm a convert now and have rented other Fields films on tape since.)

When I arrive, he tells me to help myself to anything in the small fridge, then adjourns to the bathroom. I pull out a Heineken and wait for maybe fifteen minutes before checking up on him. He sits on the edge of the tub, having some difficulty shooting up and asks if I'll pull tight the belt wrapped around his arm. I stand behind him and tug the initialized buckle. A small cloud of blood from his arm smokes into the needle before he forces it back down the vein. This scene is reflected in the mirrored wall: Ed, his head bent forward to study the needle, his shiny scalp under wisps of thinning hair, me in my NYPD uniform, a thin clean-shaven face, one hand with long fingers resting on his naked shoulder.

"What is it?" I ask.

"Crystal. There's more on the counter; help yourself." I chop the pinkish stones into powder and snort a small portion with a rolled-up bill. It helps cure pee shyness and makes me more verbal. That's the part I have the most trouble with, dirty talk. Hurting men physically, I enjoy, but I'm not much of a talker without the help of drugs or alcohol. Why is it the words that turn us on are the most absurd? "You wanna chew on this cop meat, loser?" What's so dominant about talking like someone who is emotionally dysfunctional?

Back in the bedroom I use the belt he shot up with to whip his ass. "Stick yer stink pussy in the air like a bitch in heat, loser." Eventually I swing the buckle end down on him and stamp E. T. (backward) on his right cheek. Then I have to piss. I do so, taking advantage of the fact that he's not looking. Feeding scenes are the hardest. Sexually, the idea turns me on, but I have to be real drunk to whiz while someone has my dick in his mouth. The person always looks up at you with these eyes that are trying to be subservient—*Oh yes, sir, give me your piss, sir*—but they just look impatient. I piss on his ass and back, which arches immediately in excitement. It's Ed's preference to do it on the bed instead of in the bathroom. I feel for the chambermaid.

Mike, the Patient

Mike has three children: six, five, and three years old. The older two play in the backseat while he calls from his car phone. Between dropping them off with the sitter and going to work, he comes by for a general physical. An icy stethoscope flat against the flesh just under his shoulder blade lets me hear the music of blood and chemicals. The staccato rhythm of his heart, driven to work harder by the powder he snorted while still parked outside his kid's baby-sitter's house is met with the slower, stuttered rhythm of his breathing. Such a soft, wet, noisy world, crowded with functions. Mike is paying to have me enter, with all the authority of a government agent, and disrupt these functions, which are linked in a deplorable conspiracy. They plot to keep him standing, feeding oxygen and blood to the brain so it can continue to mishandle and pervert relationships. He'd prefer to swoon and falter, to play, for a change, the victim of this flesh driven to excess. He's excited at the notion of a professional sparking rebellion among his senses.

How I actually get him to faint—or, failing this, at least make him, for a time, forget himself—is my business (literally), but the first part of our session is highly scripted. *In examining him, I discover he's involved in questionable activity. His anus is stretched beyond normal excreting functions, and he has the general health of a person who uses cocaine recreationally while partaking in debauched acts. I've seen these symptoms before, though usually among the overdeveloped set (the muscle boys of Chelsea: gays!). When I question him about it, I can see it's a point of great shame, so I use this information against him. If he allows me to run a series of experimental tests, I keep my findings secret. He agrees.*

He gets a hard-on from such phrases as, *we'll need to put you under* and *there are, of course, no guarantees* and *invasive surgery* and *we're losing him.*

Rudy and His Lover

His tiny apartment is an unsettled, but familiar, compromise between the homey kitsch of a roadside diner and a Hollywood dungeon. Leather pillows rest on the sofa, draped in an old quilt. On the tiled counter that separates the kitchen area from the rest of the room lies a set of handcuffs, a ball gag, and ceramic salt and pepper shakers shaped like two cartoonish Dutch children. They are bent forward as if to kiss each other, but here their passion is interrupted by the bottle of amyl nitrate perched between them. I've seen this aesthetic in leather bars across the globe. Dark wood paneling decorated with posters of blue-collar workers and rusty scrap metal from disassembled motorcycles are forced to share their domain with piggy-shaped plush toys and the girlish chatter of the bar's clientele.

Rudy insists we do our scene without a safe word.

"So even if you start begging for me to stop, even if you cry and scream for your life, I should ignore you and do what I please?"

"Well, . . . sort of . . . yeah. I can't get excited if I know there's an out. I-I-I wanna be thoroughly degraded and used, and part of that for me is being afraid."

"Fine," I say, "But it'll cost more, and I'll need it up front—just in case." If a guy really wants to be scared, go for his pocketbook.

Round and furry, with eyes popping out of his head, Rudy is an attention-hungry guinea pig. Normally I start light, be it pain or humiliation, and work up, testing limits as I go, but I've heard stories about Rudy from other sex workers. My friend Jeff beat up Rudy in a dark parking lot, then "stole" his wallet as part of the scene. Rudy was so thrilled, he booked another session the following week. That's uncommon—Rudy's the sort who prefers variety. In Jeff's trick diary, a little reference book listing each john's kinks and habits, Rudy is followed by the words "high threshold." As soon as he puts the money on the kitchen counter, I bring the meat of both palms down hard on his chest, knocking him to the floor. "You pathetic fuck! (etc.)" I kick his ass, literally, and the fat of his thighs, as he cowers with a giveaway grin on his face. I punch, slap, and boot him, yank his beard, and belt whip him, careful to avoid the soft spots (gut and face). Then I hog tie him and give the apartment a cursory search for clues: information to use against him, fetish toys, porn, mail with his name on it (sometimes the johns will give an alias).

Everything he wants me to find is laid out waiting on the bed: a small flogger, some paddles, leather restraints, a tub of Crisco, and far too many dildos. The dildos are lined up like soldiers, running from smallest to largest, the last in line being a gleaming black double-headed thing thicker than my arm and tipping off the edge of both sides of the queen-size mattress. There's also a dog collar, a Polaroid camera, and some underpants that say, *Shit Happens.*

In the corner of the room is tattoo equipment: a gun and several inks. I assume it's his line of work but find out the tat stuff belongs to the man whose photo is stuck on the refrigerator, Rudy's lover, presently at a convention in Georgia. The photograph shows a tall man, younger than Rudy, but similar in looks. He's bare-chested and intricately decorated with tat work. I proceed to beat Rudy more for cheating. "When's he back?" I demand. "I wanna know how long to make the bruises last. You're gonna have a lot of explaining to do." Until now, Rudy's pretty much taken everything without resistance, but when I threaten him with his own boyfriend, the wheels of panic start turning. He cranes his thick neck in my direction. His eyebrows lift and beg. Having hit a nerve, it's important to keep at it. I pull the clippers from my bag. "Please!" he says, worming his rope-bound flesh back along the floor. His fat makes squeaks and sucking sounds against the linoleum.

"Please, *what?*"

"Please, I don't care if you hurt me physically, but please, don't let my boyfriend find out." He's begging. The guy who insisted on doing away with a safe word is begging.

"No," I slap the cord of the clippers against the kitchen floor like a whip, "the proper phrase is, *please, SIR.*"

It's midafternoon outside, but this apartment is sealed into perpetual night. A macramé owl, gray with dust, looks down at us with acorn eyes. Next to that, a framed photo, cut from a magazine, of a muscular, naked man curled into the womb of a fallen tree.

Mike and Mr. Leather Daddy

On his sixth visit, Mike, the Patient, brings a present: an old black-and-white photograph of a hospital, the word *Emergency* readable backward on a glass door in the background. In the foreground is a man who looks to have been in a fight; his head droops forward and blood from his mouth and nose covers his shirt front. He's held standing by a second man in a black cap and sweater vest.

This man is saying something, almost shouting at his injured friend, the muscles of his jaw stretched taut. These words clearly make no sense to the bloodied man, though it's possible he at least hears the tone of encouragement. The third figure, a doctor in a long white coat, moves toward the couple with his body but, at the same time, looks back over his shoulder at something out of the frame. It is amazing, the urgency expressed in his body as he hurries to the bloodied man, and the focused intensity of his expression as he listens to the last bit of some instruction, or tells another patient with his eyes, *I'll be with you, soon.*

I planned to give Mike an enema, but he's an hour late and I've got Grandma scheduled next, a trip across town. "We can still do a little," he says, "If I give you a ride, you'll save some time." I should refuse, but the gift sways me. I have him naked in my tub, his wrists manacled and roped to a quick-release clamp in the ceiling. I wear a rubber mitt while slapping his chest and threaten him with the words that tortured Sally Field in the movie *Sybil.*

Hold your water.

After the scene, we hurry out to his car. To make room, he removes the child seat and tosses it in the trunk. The sight of this makes his children more real to me than their voices ever had, or perhaps it's that now I can place those voices in a context: a Lincoln Mercury, the two older kids fighting over the Gameboy in the backseat, the baby strapped into its chair on the passenger side.

I study his present again—not sure why I brought it—the doctor's handsome face, something (a pen?) in his left hand. On the back, *April 1947,* in elegant script, as well as a joke, *You should see the other guy!*

Next month, Mike's wife and kids will visit her parents for two weeks over spring break—*will that be long enough for the marks to heal?* It's a short drive, but in the course of it, these marks swell and multiply. Using the photograph as muse, he wants me to play several parts in one: the brute who beats him, the friend who carries him, the doctor who repairs him. *If I hit him hard in the face,* he promises, *his nose will bleed a lot. If I cut him, I can put in stitches; he has access to the right kind of thread and needles—that would be intense. If I break something, a finger maybe, I can set it with gauze and plaster. Do I know how to do that?*

His vision of my control is laced with nurturing. My friend Jeff says it's my calm that brings this out in people. We laugh about the (off-duty) date I had with one of the Mr. Leather Daddies. I was tired of always doing all the work, and this guy had been after me for a while to bottom for him, so one day I agreed. In the past, when looking to be topped, I went for beefy, mean-looking guys who talked a good show. But, these guys were always too quick to show me their softer side. "I feel like I can do this with you," they'd say, lifting their muscled thighs to accommodate my 140 pounds of man flesh. This Daddy however relied more on a long reputation than intimidating looks. He had history under, and on, his belt. At his house, he had me strip and explain what I was doing there. The disorientation alone sent a rush of adrenaline. My dick started to stiffen. I put my hands behind my back, eyes down. "I'm here for your pleasure, Sir."

"That's good," he chuckled. "But before we launch into it, why don't you relax and give me some details. What do you like?"

Negotiations. I gave him my story, *not much experience bottom-ing, but a good knowledge of how-to from the other side of the fence, blah, blah, blah. . . .* By the time I was done, he looked me deep in the eyes and told me he understood because *he never bottomed* anymore, never felt like he could with any of the tops he knew, but I had a really strong, exciting energy and . . .

I'm no Tom of Finland drawing; the closest I come to a macho archetype is a stern male librarian, so I suppose I should be grateful for this "energy." Granted, if I insisted on being the bottom, I'm sure he would've accommodated, but the idea of topping that year's "big top" was too inviting. I went for it—even though I'm sure it's just a story he uses to hook suckers like me.

Once, Mike asked if I ever bottomed. For most clients, the answer would be a simple no, but Mike and I had built a strong rapport. I told him, "I try to stay open to all experiences, but no, not lately." For Mike, I'm not so much a "top" as an authority figure. I'm a disapproving caretaker, nursing wounds with frequent shakes of the head and cutting reprimands.

You didn't fall down any stairs. Someone beat you! Who? Who did this to you? One of your drug dealers? One of your so-called friends at those queer bars you visit? One of those sleazy male hustlers you hire to stick things up your rectum?

Rudy and Manuel

Manuel, though it's probably not his real name, is standing in line for the toilet at this hustler bar. At twenty-two, he's the oldest boy here, not counting myself and the obvious johns. Except for a goatee, he looks a lot like Victor, the guy in Grandma's scrapbook, down to a preference for silver jewelry: one chain around his neck and about four rings. We share a drink before returning to the scene of the crime—Rudy's money in my pocket while Rudy waits in his dark apartment, kneeling on my word that I'll bring him back "something." Manuel asks questions related to our shared profession: *Do I do well with an ad? How much do I charge if a guy just wants to blow me?* Then we share more detailed stories. I chose Manuel because I find him attractive. I never bought a hustler before, but it isn't long before I'm thinking like a john, wondering *if we might have some connection.*

With a job like this, it's impossible to find a boyfriend. I've often thought that with another hustler, things could work. I don't expect anything romantic to happen between Manuel and me, but thinking about it makes him more exciting, makes the job easier.

Moving lights make the bar appear to breathe. We have two drinks, but when I stand, my knees remind me this is on an empty stomach. An already narrow space becomes crowded with the first wave of happy hour. The marbled mirror interior tightens like a lung in slow exhale. I move toward the door, Manuel in tow.

I say, "Just one stop first."

Around the corner from the bar, there's an old gentleman's shop. Inside, the clerk nods and smiles. He retrieves a hefty shopping bag from behind the counter and says, "They're all wrapped."

"Thanks, but actually I have one more errand and need to add a last gift, could you hold them one more hour?" Father's Day is around the corner so I bought presents for the men in my life: Dad, my pal Jeff, my brother, even one for Grandma, and three for myself: expensive, fussy, mannish things—handkerchiefs and engraved flasks, shaving kits, a money clip. "I'd like the chain after all, the thicker silver one. I'm glad I found this shop; you saved a lot of footwork. I never noticed it before." The clerk beams as if the compliments were about him. He leans forward, flirtatiously dropping his stiff posture. "It is nice, isn't it?" he says. "Do you want to put this on your credit card again?"

Manuel's eyes are on me as I hand the clerk the American Express Card. I had fished it from the back of a drawer in Rudy's bedside table, exactly where I knew it would be. When Jeff talked about the incident in the parking lot, he mentioned Rudy's wallet was empty of credit cards and ID, just a wad of cash that wasn't much more than what Jeff would've been paid anyway. "If I hadn't mugged him, he would've been sorely disappointed. The guy planned on it."

I never stole from a client before, but this is also my first scene without a safe word. It gives things a boundlessness; if Rudy has no limits, why should I? I forge his signature a second time and shake my head when the clerk asks if I want this wrapped as well.

"Thanks, no, I'll take it with me."

Returning to Rudy's, I brace Manuel once more for what awaits us. I gave the pig a drastic makeover: his head and facial hair shaved save for a Hitler 'stache and two short Heidi-like braids curling up like parenthetical marks containing his worried brain (uh-oh!). With iodine, I painted a target on his large stomach, and his eyebrows are pinned up with temporary piercing needles. All this, sandwiched around his already bulging eyes, gives him a look of permanent shock.

"You cut off the mohawk," says Manuel, referring to a Polaroid I showed him at the bar, one of Rudy in midtransition.

"Say hello to Manuel," I instruct. Rudy drops to his knees to lick the newcomer's boots, revealing whip marks on his back. I kick him. "Don't get your filthy spit on the top of his boots." Manuel catches on immediately and adds, "Yeah, lick the tread, *bendejo!*" We both roll our eyes.

Two Sides

Isadora Stern

There was a time when I talked to men who went to peep shows; they called me as part of the process—the confessions of their sins as titillating as the crime itself. I was paid to listen, in that time, to their fears: The AIDS that surely lurked close in their future for having gone against what was moral and right. For, in the height of passion, in all the excitement, in their need to be close, they had licked the glass. They had licked the glass that kept them from being too close to the girl they desired so much. They had licked the glass as if it were a permeable membrane and it could transmit the taste of the girl just on the other side. They had licked the glass, and in the hours that followed, their minds became clouded with shame.

Licking the glass at the jack shack is not a good idea. Because of the AIDS. Because the AIDS is dirty and so is the jack shack. And when you are dirty, and get off in dirty ways, you get what you deserve.

AIDS education on the hotline was all about shame. They called with shameful questions, and we relieved their fears with fact. They called with bigoted assumptions, and we shamed them into changing their minds. They called because they knew that they had been dirty and dirty people got the AIDS, seeing as the fags are being dirty for ass fucking, and now these guys were dirty for masturbating in public; they had sunk as low as the ass man and gotten the AIDS themselves.

Do not feed or tease the fearful. Why, in this world, am I the one being kind to these men?

"Okay, first you would become infected with HIV; you would not contract AIDS immediately. . . . Now, you were at the peep show and you licked the glass, and that is your only possible exposure to HIV?"

"Yes, I licked the glass, and that was six months ago, and I've had diarrhea ever since, and I'm losing weight and I can't sleep and I get tested every month, and it's always negative, and when will it show I have the AIDS?!"

Why can't fear and ignorance be deadly? Why is it that his good time won't kill him?

"Sir, you are suffering from anxiety. Your guilt over your behavior of licking the glass at peep shows is making you sick, not HIV or AIDS. Let me suggest a place where you can talk about this more . . .

* * *

There was a time when I talked to men who went to peep shows. They came into the booth and took the brave step of taking the quarter out of their pocket; they took the final shameful step and made the window rise. Now we, the dancers, could see them, and they, the men, could feel close to the pretty dancing girls.

There was talking out of their mouths, but due to the thickness of the glass and the volume of the music, I could not hear their words. I could read their lips and watch their motions. Their arms and hands told me their big wish. They hoped my cunt would magically fall open for their enjoyment. I understood their minds. The more I became simple body parts, the less guilt they had to feel when they got home. If they saw me as whole, I would eat away at their consciousness.

It is embarrassing to be devoted to women behind glass. But the men came, day after day, and spent their lunch money and stroked their cocks to get off. Their payment, mostly in the thunking sound of quarters, with a few brave ones committing to a full dollar, was for the pleasure of being near the pretty girls.

Gazing down, I followed the same pattern at each window: window went up, I made eye contact, I wandered over slowly. I ran through my tricks; I used the muscles I didn't know I had. And I watched the men. Sometimes I would really watch. I would stop dancing, rest my arms on the ledge of the window, tilt my head, bite my lip, and stare. I would think about their guilt. I would check for wedding rings, name tags, company logos, lube bottles, cell phones, latte cups, cameras, woman's clothing, and all the while make sexy faces. I would play the game that kept me going—I knew they had shame. More shame than I would ever have about being there. They would never tell anyone face-to-face that they pay for sex.

The customers loved my stare downs. In their reckless, abandoned desire to feel the moment, they would get as close as they could.

They would lick the glass. It wasn't tentative licking, no quick tongue darts here and there. It was full force, the way you would lick the best-tasting, most pleasurable food. Long licks, deep gazes, lots of wanting and loneliness.

"Sir, it's the dirtiest of the dirty where you are right now. Although your delusion is my paycheck, I must remind you, we are eye candy; we will not fill you. We may get you off, but you must remember we are offering you a service, brief and to the point, not a meal that can satiate you."

* * *

There was a long time in my life when I talked to the men who went to peep shows. Listening and watching, I have seen bad behavior. Reckless are these men, when they are swept away from their guilt, if only for a quarter's worth of a moment. And then guilt would return, but I would hear from them again, not so brave this time. This time shaken, remembering that sex is filth. Repeat: release, guilt, shame. Being a bad boy, just for a moment, before they have to go back to the real world. I get to sit, witness, and record.

–20–

A Complicated Business

Tony Valenzuela

Prostitution is a complicated business. At times I'm beside my-self with the ease of it all—the amount of money I make, the freedom it gives me to sit at Starbucks in West Hollywood and cruise boys anytime I want, the places I travel to, things I buy, restaurants I'm taken to. . . . And then I can't wait to get out of it, feeling like I'd rather throw myself into traffic than have to turn another trick. Hooking makes dating next to impossible, and I get frustrated that it cuts into my personal sex life.

It's a crazy, fucked-up world that I'm proud to partake in, as when I worked my ass off through college as a waiter. But this is far more special. The motivations, risks, and sacrifices are high drama. The payoff, at times, simply glamorous. The freedom has been nothing less than lifesaving. Every whore has his own story . . .

The evening I launched my career as a high-priced homosexual prostitute (as the media used to call Andrew Cunanan, the gay serial killer), I was sitting alone, painfully bored and frustrated at the part-time minimum-wage job I'd taken in a small clothing store in Hillcrest. I had just come out of the longest depression of my life, and the retail job was my reintroduction to responsibility. Two years prior, at age twenty-six, I learned I'd become HIV positive. My infection bulldozed my already crumbling idealism, and, eventual-ly, the career I'd carefully built throughout my twenties as a profes-sional gay activist collapsed. Facing one's mortality is a hard and fast lesson in cutting through bullshit. I couldn't take the rank smell of a sterilized gay movement any longer. Furthermore, the loneli-ness of the changed epidemic for someone of my generation forced

151

me into a solitary process of grieving for a life that felt destroyed, yet showed no signs of destruction—no KS lesions, no memorial services for my best friends, no surprise obituaries, not even a Quilt to help release the tears I felt guilty to shed in public.

Writing about the anguish of telling my parents, or the recurring feelings of hopelessness that I would die young, or my battle to get the gay community to understand the complexities of sexual risk taking in an evolving and unyielding epidemic—these are heavy subjects to skim over in order to have the space to recount even a slice of my career in sex work. They were experiences that consumed two dark years of my life that I pushed through with a morbid sense of humor, like belly laughing over every issue of *Diseased Pariah News* or wanting to title my first book *HIV Positive and LOVING IT!*, with a picture of an ecstatic me on the cover doing a jig. Above all, I got through that time with the loving support of a few friends and a dear, remarkable family.

I often look back at my family's history to try to pull up how its values influenced my sexual exploration. My father, who is Mexican, is a Latino through and through when it comes to sex. He was quite a playboy when he was young, and marriage didn't seem to taper his wandering libido. Observing my father, I sometimes shudder to think what kind of smooth-talking womanizer I might have become had I been straight. Instead, I was lucky enough to be part of a group of people (gay men) who view sexual conquest as a community value rather than a victory over weakness.

I was already predisposed to hustling. Sex has been a sweeping and defining theme in my life, almost epic in my adulthood. The two great crises of my life, homosexuality and HIV, both have very much to do with sex. Sex has been an obsessive fascination of mine, like food and cooking are to my mother, who is constantly poring over culinary books and magazines, always trying new recipes and perfecting old ones. She owns an Italian restaurant. I opened a one-man brothel.

My background is Third World and Old World (immigrant Mexican on my father's side, first-generation Italian on my mother's), but with a First World sense of entitlement. In other words, the Valenzuelas have made their way through America expecting everyone else to think the way we do.

"Wives need to understand the service that prostitutes provide to a marriage," my fifty-seven-year-old mother said loudly at a family gathering a couple of years back. Not to misunderstand her, my mom is actually a sexual prude. One time she asked me what a ménage à trois was, and when I told her, she responded, wide-eyed and horrified, "That's disgusting!" But she's also wise to the world of Monica Lewinsky and Bill Clinton. When I told her nervously that I'd made my first porn movie, the first thing she asked was how much money I got for it. She has a strong live-and-let-live attitude about most things, even with her children.

"I've never met a prostitute I didn't like," she stated with conviction, as the rest of the family munched on chips and seviche.

"Neither has Dad!" my sister screamed. We all roared with laughter.

In situations such as these with my family, I think it's no wonder I am how I am. And it's no wonder I'm a snag in the fabric of rigid values in American society. To live honestly about one's sexual desires and behaviors is an assault to most people who unabashedly lie about their sex lives and sexual fantasies.

That fateful evening at the clothing store, I was resolved to simplify my life economically and venture into sex work, which had long been a burning curiosity. I decided that I would drive up to LA and check out the fabled hooker bar Numbers, where several of my friends had met their sugar daddies. To avoid the hassle of anyone trying to talk me out of this decision, I began my profession without telling a soul. I didn't know where the bar was, so I dialed Los Angeles information for the number. I realized I couldn't ask if this was the bar where hustlers hooked up with clients, so I said to the man who answered the phone, "I'm calling from San Diego, and is this the bar that has that *very interesting reputation* for its clientele?" "Yes, it is," he answered, with a chuckle. I asked for directions.

After a two-hour drive up from San Diego, I arrived at Numbers, which was then on Sunset Boulevard, at around 10:30 p.m. I didn't even know what to wear or how the procedure worked. I kept telling myself that I wouldn't be ashamed if I ran into anyone I knew, though I prayed that I wouldn't. Like all of my escort friends, I made up a pseudonym. Although I didn't understand making up a name for something that required me being seen, I made one up anyway. I came up with "Marco" because I look Mediterranean and because it seemed exotic and sexy.

I parked my car a couple of blocks away from the bar. Still sitting in the driver's seat, I pulled on skintight black vinyl pants and a tight black shirt. A hustler should look like a hustler, I thought. In truth, one of my sexual fantasies was to feel like a hooker. I would soon realize how much I got off on the idea of being bought, being someone's piece of ass for an hour or an evening. It was a turn-on, especially when the client treated me like "his whore." ("Do as I say you little faggot whore!" or "Suck my dick pussy boy!") Unfortunately, I'd learn that most clients weren't into playing my cheap hooker fantasy scenes. It was about them, not me. Though, often-times, they'd tell me it was important I was getting pleasure also ("Oh, of course. It feels great . . ." I'd say as I left my body).

Numbers had smoked-glass mirrored walls as you walked in, with a bathroom immediately to the right. I checked myself out in the full length of the mirrors, turning around to inspect my butt. I stopped in the restroom to kill a little time. The restroom was tiny and crowded, and it was completely obvious who would be buying and who would be selling downstairs at the bar. I waited my turn for the mirror. As everyone stared at me, I self-consciously looked at the whites of my eyes, my teeth, fussed a bit with my hair.

There was a young guy, one of the hookers, I presumed, at the urinal talking to an older man who was peering over his shoulder at the guy's dick, commenting on its enormous size. Two other men took a peek, and the younger guy peeing seemed to enjoy the attention. A disturbing feeling of embarrassment came over me, like he was a white-trash prostitute for letting them look. All the while, I wanted to look, too, but didn't, and I was no better, wearing pants so tight anyone could tell I wasn't wearing underwear.

With my heart pounding hard in my chest, I walked down the flight of stairs that descended into the bar. I'd forgotten that Numbers was also a restaurant. It was dimly lit and smoky. The floor was jammed with young guys and older men, either standing around or sitting at the tables that surrounded the bar area. It took about one minute for me to run into someone from San Diego, who, by his age and outfit, was obviously there selling. I sucked in my disconcerted surprise and walked over to say hello.

"It's my first time here. How does this work?" I asked.

He looked at me with a "yeah, right" expression on his face and said, smiling, "Yeah, right."

"No, I'm not telling you that to, like, say that I don't do this. I'm really serious. I've never been here before." I pleaded for him to believe me.

I remembered this guy from back home. He used to sing occasionally at one of the Hillcrest coffeehouses with live entertainment. I always thought he had a beautiful voice, kind of high for a man, like George Michael's. He was attractive, but small and thin.

He instructed me to stand around in different parts of the bar and try to make eye contact with people. "Someone is bound to lock eyes with you, and if he does, walk over and say hello. Or they might wave you over, or have a drink sent over to you. The going rate is $150 here. Try not to spend too much time in conversation so that you can be out of here as soon as possible." He looked me up and down and said, "You won't have any trouble here, doll, especially in those pants."

I bought myself a Cape Cod and positioned myself at one end of the bar so that I could observe the crowd. I felt more at ease tucked away in a dark corner, though I realized I needed to make myself visible. I was incredibly relieved that I hadn't spotted anyone else I knew. After about twenty minutes of standing and looking around, I noticed an obese, dark-haired man sitting at the bar who kept looking over at me, then down at his cocktail. I locked eyes with him until he waved me over. I swaggered toward him, bluffing a confident look.

I introduced myself as "Marco." His name was Joe. He said he'd never seen me before. I told him I wasn't from LA and that this was my first time at the bar. He said I looked new. I didn't know what he meant by that, but all of a sudden, I felt embarrassed that I wore skintight black vinyl pants. In the middle of this small-talk conversation, a man walked up to us to greet Joe. He was the owner of the bar. I introduced myself to him as "Tony," immediately realizing, before that second syllable escaped my lips, that I'd made my first hooker faux pas. He gave me an enthusiastic "Nice to meet you, Tony!" squeezing my knee, and continued on to his other owner responsibilities.

I clumsily rambled my way through an explanation for why I told Joe my name was "Marco." He didn't seem to care. I felt like a complete moron. I kept thinking what my San Diego friend said, "Don't spend too much time talking." But, as would be customary of me throughout my career as an escort, I would break all the rules, even ones that were supposed to benefit me.

We became engaged in conversation. He was an artist. Numbers was his hangout. He bought only occasionally but liked that I didn't have that "professional hustler" look, like most of the others. Much later, when I would acquire that look at the bar, I would call it the "Don't even think of bullshitting me" look. Joe had a very gentle, homely look, as if he were the kind of man who, at forty-five, was still living with his mother. I told him I was a writer and was looking to find new ways to support myself. For nearly an hour we talked about writing, living in LA, good movies—I was enjoying myself.

"So . . ." I said to Joe, as a cue to move our conversation to its next logical step.

"What would it cost to have you come to my apartment?" he asked softly, though not nervously, like I would later hear from not-so-regular Numbers customers.

"A hundred and fifty dollars," I said, thankful that my friend had informed me of the market price. I wondered what I might have said otherwise. I wasn't good at driving a hard bargain.

"That seems to be the standard here," he said calmly, and agreed to hire.

We both got up from the bar stools at the same time and walked through the crowd and up the staircase together. I felt a burning heat of stares, as if we were wearing bright neon hats that flashed HOOKER and JOHN, with arrows pointing at our heads.

A Year and a Half Later . . .

I met a guy at that fabulous LA den of depravity called the Probe. He had purple spiked hair, piercings in his ears, nipples, and belly button, and a tanned body so perfectly proportioned and defined, he looked as if he'd been skillfully painted into the atmosphere. His unique style in a room full of beauty clones caught my attention. We flirted on and off for about an hour, though his interest in me seemed undecided. After I realized he wasn't interested in hooking up that evening, I went to the bar and wrote on a piece of paper, "You're a beautiful boy," with my phone number. I handed it to him and asked him to call me so I could take him out.

I'd dated only one guy, Gary (for very short time), in the year and a half since becoming an escort. The week I met him, in the summer of 1997, I was shooting *Positively Yours*, the historic porno flick that was the first to tackle the subject of HIV, with the first ever openly HIV-positive model, myself. While I was proud of these claims to fame, I lied to my new flame by telling him I had family obligations and so, therefore, couldn't see him during the weekend. By this point, dating Tony Valenzuela came to mean surviving my one-two-three punch: HIV-Positive–Porn Star–Prostitute.

Immediately, I felt guilty about lying, so I called Gary back and told him the truth about my porn movie role and then disclosed my HIV status. He, too, was positive and had only slight reservations about seeing a "porn star," but not enough to stop seeing me on the spot. It wasn't until a week later, after deciding that keeping this information from him was misleading, that I revealed my true profession through a carefully crafted e-mail. His reaction was fairly supportive, and he had a million questions about the nature of the business. But soon after, the romance fizzled, and, to this day, I'm not completely sure why, even though Gary and I have become close friends. I never had the guts to come out and say, "So, was it because I'm a hooker?"

Since Gary, I hadn't dated another guy. I'd moved to Los Angeles about a year into my call boy career, which was proving to be financially successful. As much as escorting had become a regular job to me, with a number of great repeat clients whom had genuinely become my friends, and the mindless routine that everyone has in every job, I understood that most people, even gay men, considered the profession contemptible. While I can very well distinguish sex for money from sex with a romantic interest, most guys cannot. Even "open-minded" men draw the line at *dating* an escort. So to save myself the hurt of rejection or insult, I'd closed myself to romance.

But this purple-haired original mesmerized me, and I couldn't resist asking him out. He called me the following afternoon, much to my surprise. We had a pleasant conversation on the phone about his hair stylist career, my activist background, and why I moved to Los Angeles. We made a date to meet that evening for a drink at Marix, an overcrowded Sunday night hangout in West Hollywood. While a part of me was taking the evening casually, another part of me was hopeful. I regretted that dating felt near to impossible for an escort. So why even bother, I fretted.

After arriving at the restaurant and ordering margaritas on the rocks, we found a place to stand and continued the "getting to know you" we'd started on the phone that afternoon. We covered the basics: work, family, drugs, what we thought of each other when we first met at Probe. He told me he actually would not have considered going out with me because I looked like one of those "typical" Probe guys, but that he was impressed by the way I asked him out. "No one says 'I'd like to take you out' anymore," he said. "It's always, 'Here's my number. Call me.'"

"There's a lot about me that's surprising," I said. Over the course of an hour and a half and three strong margaritas, we were having a lovely, almost intimate conversation within the shoulder-to-shoulder confines of Marix. He excused himself to go to the bathroom, and I sat debating when to deliver my one-two-three punch. I could skip the porn star part, I thought. If he can handle HIV and prostitution, he's likely to consider porn a virtue in comparison. But is it necessary to tell him now? Is it inappropriate and presumptuous?

The tequila was swimming through my bloodstream like underwater ballet dancers. I felt warm and contented. I felt like telling him and not having to preoccupy myself between now and date number two with the anxiety of disclosure. After all, at that point, I wasn't that invested, and I was looking for a man in my life who had a broad enough mind and a strong enough character to accept prostitution for what it is—my livelihood.

He came back to our little space, and this is what I said: "You know how you told me your impression of me changed by the way I asked you out? Well, there are some other things I need to tell you that might seem surprising also, considering what you know about me already."

When I'm nervous, and I was terribly nervous, I speak quickly and I ramble. "The first thing is that I'm HIV positive. I've been positive for three and a half years, but I'm healthy, and I take medications, which I'm doing really well on. Some guys aren't comfortable to be with someone who's positive, which I understand, so I wanted you to know that now." I was absorbed in my testimony, more concerned with getting the words out clearly than gauging his response.

I thought we would probably have sex later that night. Not that I always disclose my HIV status before sex, but with the degree of intimacy we were establishing, I didn't want any nasty surprises. I'd recently hooked up with a twenty-four-year-old at the Roxy in New York City. We hadn't even had sex, and when I told him I was HIV positive, he freaked out because we'd been kissing for several hours.

I continued, "About a year and a half ago, I decided I needed to find a way to support myself that allowed me to pursue my goals as a writer. So, what I did was tried out being an *escort*." I emphasized escort so he would understand the broader context under which I was using the word. "And it worked out really well. So, that's how I make my living. While I do all those other things I've told you about, like writing and activism, my main source of income is as an escort." I hated feeling like I needed to counter my "good" qualities with the "vice" of my profession.

Throughout my confessional, he stared at me with an expression that looked neither accepting nor critical. I took in a breath and said, "That's it. . . . *Sooo* . . ." I laughed nervously.

He paused for a moment, then began, "I told you my impression of you switched by the way you asked me out. Well, it's completely switched back to what I first thought of you." I was taken aback by his sharp tone. "Do you really expect that I would go out with you knowing what you just told me? I mean, the HIV part I understand because I think you should say something. But the escort part? Doesn't that just mean male prostitute?"

I was stunned at his almost cruel delivery, though unflinching and calm in my response, "Yes it does. You know, I don't expect anyone to go out with me knowing I'm an escort, but I do conceive of the idea of guys existing who would."

I saw our date spiraling downward in a fiery ball. I was wondering if I would have to walk home or if he would still drive me home after this confrontation. But all of a sudden, as blunt as his initial reaction had been, his tone softened.

"I said to you earlier that I'm not a judgmental person." He was referring to our discussion about drugs and how he doesn't generally use them, but doesn't care if others do. "It's all okay with me, everything you just told me. It's all fine." He grabbed my knee and smiled.

I didn't understand what had just occurred in his head to inspire his change of heart. His temperament seemed humble now. With such an instantaneous turnaround in opinion, I thought he'd remembered something in his own past that smacked him in the face with hypocrisy. But I was speculating, and I didn't feel like asking. Several days later, when I did ask about his "360" turn in opinion, he apologized, admitting he was shocked by my news. He told me he just as quickly resolved that he wasn't going to let his prejudices intercept what might be meeting a "great" person.

It's interesting the trust you gain from people when you divulge sensitive personal information. The first-date insecurities that kept us from touching each other in a demonstrative fashion melted away. After taking the conversation in a lighter direction for a while, we left Marix holding hands and headed for Mickey's.

Some people might think I should not have tolerated his initial condemnation. But I felt like I'd told him something truly unexpected and out of the ordinary. I was, by then, used to accommodating others for my peculiar life's experiences by cutting them some slack, but only at first. Everyone deserves a chance to prove their character.

At one point, a couple of hours later, while we were on the dance floor at Mickey's, he stopped, looked me in the eyes, and said, "You were incredible back at the restaurant, being so completely honest with me."

I will never forget those words. Regardless of whether I dated him for only a short time or ended up marrying him, in one sentence, he gratified the intense labor of honesty I've ventured to pursue, not only with him, but throughout my life. It's odd and amazing to me how such a small gesture of understanding made me feel like bursting into tears. I contained my emotions and hugged him, kissing his neck.

21

Payment by Donation:
Every Sperm Is Sacred

David Porter

What if a client offered you fifty dollars to go to his place, masturbate alone in a private room with ample porn magazines, and then leave as soon as you orgasmed? What if you could come back two to three times a week to earn over four hundred and fifty dollars a month for at least a year?

Sound enticing?

What if I told you the same client also would have a keen interest in vampirism and water sports, and, hence, would poke you with needles to draw blood and also make you pee for him? What if he was obsessed with your health and made you answer hundreds of questions about your personal and familial medical history? He would keep considerable data on you, including your Social Security number and all the results of the various tests he would conduct on you.

Welcome to the life of a sperm donor. In recent years, as bio-technology has developed and infertile and lesbian couples pursue their various options, considerable attention has been paid to the issues raised by sperm donation. But most of the cultural texts produced on this topic focus on either the experiences of the woman or the couple receiving the sperm, or on the relationship (or lack thereof) between the child and the donor dad.

In my work as a sperm donor, I could talk endlessly about those issues and my feelings about being the genetic father of children I will never raise and maybe never even meet. But what fascinates me most about the topic of sperm donation is the experience of the workers themselves. After all, sperm banking is a highly profitable, rapidly expanding branch of the biotechnology industry.

Most aspects of the sex industry (e.g., prostitution, stripping, dancing, modeling, etc.) promote the recreational, pleasurable side of sex for the client, as opposed to the procreative side. Those recreational clients do not care if the worker has a family history of heart disease, has type O+ blood or a low sperm count, as long as the worker can provide the physical or visual pleasure requested by the client. Thus, sex work is a performance, and the primary positive lasting result is the exchange of money.

Unlike most sex industry clients, the client in the case of sperm donation is solely interested in the end results. The worker is paid, not to masturbate, but to ejaculate a quality "specimen." The come is to be placed in vials, stored in containers marked "biohazard," and carefully studied to determine its suitability for impregnating. The positive lasting results of this process are both the exchange of money and, ideally, a healthy child.

In this industry, a high sperm count is valued far more than a big dick. You need not only be reasonably attractive and HIV negative but also must have a family history free of disease, pass a doctor's physical, and submit to frequent and thorough tests of blood and urine that may indicate you have viruses and bacteria you didn't even know existed.

All of this amounts to an intense screening process. No one has an inherent right to be a donor. I couldn't even sleep with the boss to get the job. With all the recent debates over affirmative action, this is a job where what you are genetically is all that matters. Obviously, you have to be male, but you also have to be a younger male (under forty). We've all seen the adoption ads insisting on "white newborns" only, so you can imagine the lack of demand for babies of color through sperm donation. Forget it if you have a disability of any kind or a history of disability in your family. It certainly helps to be smart, tall, and attractive. (No fats, no fems.) Be prepared to answer questions about ethnic origin, religion, alcohol and drug use, and any sexual experiences you have had that put you in the so-called risk categories for HIV.

With all of that said, in this prostituting society, we all have to hustle. When I passed all of the requirements previously outlined, I found it difficult to turn down the job just because it discriminates against others. In an industry that thrives on power and desire, if I had what they wanted and they were willing to pay, I thought, I might as well go for it unless the risks or harm were too great.

When I tell my friends that one of the ways I support my survival in the capitalist system is sperm donating, they are greatly amused. After all, what could be more empowering than getting paid fifty bucks to do what millions of horny men do for free every day because they want to? Ever since our first sexual awakenings, it has been an almost universally held truth among men in this society that jerking off is easy and fun to do.

It blows people's minds that I could walk into work, pull down my pants, look at porn, have an orgasm and come in a cup, and walk out a few minutes later, fifty dollars richer. By minimum wage standards, it would take almost ten hours of painfully boring work to earn that same amount of money.

Even if you are earning more than minimum wage, the money has its appeal. Prior to becoming a sperm donor, I tended bar one night a week to earn extra money. It was a noisy, smoky, dirty college hangout that catered primarily to the fake-ID, under-twenty-one crowd. My shift started at 9 p.m., the place closed at one, and by 2 a.m., after cleaning and mopping the vomit, the night would finally be over. I'd come home reeking of beer and smoke but proud of the thirty dollars in tips in my pocket. Combined with my base wage, a night's work earned me a little over fifty dollars. My first few weeks as a sperm donor, just thinking about this change of fortune in the economics of my life was enough to get me off.

With all of that said, as with many sex industry jobs, sperm donation has the potential to tinker with the very core of your sexuality. First, it is important to note that in order to produce the best-quality sperm, the donor must ejaculate two to three days before ejaculating at the sperm bank. Thus, depending on how desperate I am for money, a significant part of the week can be tied up in the ejaculation-abstinence cycle.

All parts of this cycle cause problems. First is the difficulty of having to write "come" in my appointment book three days before going to the bank. If I am alone on the specified day, imagine the feeling of having to masturbate, no matter how busy you are or how little you want to. Once, I completely forgot until I was at work at my regular, daytime, forty-hours-a-week job and had to sneak into the bathroom to meet my ejaculation requirement. Now, to some readers, I realize that the idea of masturbating at work is an appealing idea—a break from the tedium of their jobs. But the thrill wasn't there when it became part of my job description. I looked at the clock and realized time was ticking by, and if I didn't come soon, my sperm count might be low. All specimens were put under a microscope; those with low counts were paid less, and, over time, consistently lower counts meant being fired. If I am with a partner on a given day, I have to turn to my partner and say, in effect, "I must come now, no matter what mood you are in. If you are uninterested, I can do it on my own." Sometimes my partner is more than willing: we joke about a fifty-dollar charge for each time that I come. The experience gives me a renewed appreciation for the come shot in porn flicks.

In the middle of a cycle, I have to be keenly aware and effectively stifle any desire to come, whether that be alone, with a horny partner, or, unknowingly, in a wet dream. Finally, at the end of the cycle, I have to bring myself to orgasm while standing up, with my penis pointed downward (so it will go in the cup), in a small, sterile room. In this environment, although there are no time limits articulated, it certainly does not hurt to be fast. I have to overcome any anxiety that might make me lose my erection or become totally impotent. As with many professionals, I want to excel at my job. I entertain myself by seeing how quickly I can come. Sometimes I'm there less than thirty seconds before semen is pumping through my hard cock and into the plastic cup. When I am not at work, however, my sexual partners are expecting more than thirty seconds of thrusting. Balancing the different skills required at work versus at home can be difficult in any career path.

It is amazing how quickly one's sexuality can stagnate when such a cycle is followed week after week. Masturbation can be a preteen boy's favorite hobby, but it can also be an adult male's most alienating labor. On the job, I am profoundly alone. In an era when schoolteachers and business leaders are touting the value of collaborative work, producing sperm in America is unlikely to become a group project. Sometimes, to entertain myself, I imagine a circle jerk of sperm donation. An entire breeder class could report to work in the morning.

One of the aspects I have enjoyed the most about other places I have worked is the sense of community and camaraderie with my fellow workers. The dullest of jobs can be made bearable by interesting co-workers. As a sperm donor, not only have I never been introduced to my co-workers, I do not know who they are. I know less about them than the people who buy our sperm.

On rare occasions, I have accidentally passed one of my co-workers in the sperm bank. I know this is only by mistake because our appointments are carefully scheduled so as not to overlap. The other donors refuse to look me in the eye, much less shake my hand. I guess a certain stigma still surrounds masturbation and selling come.

Thus, on any given workday, there is just the management and me. They take my blood and store my sperm, but they are just middlemen between the donors and the purchasers of the end product. There are no holiday parties, just tattered pages of porn magazines with images that hundreds of men fantasized about as they came.

Sperm donation is a relatively new industry. It comes in a late capitalist era when the social, technological, and medical aspects of it are significantly advanced enough in their own right to allow it to happen. Like phone sex, it provides a certain amount of anonymity, only made possible by technology. And like cybersex, it is only possible because of advanced technology. Your home ice cube tray wasn't designed for freezing sperm.

The industry is also coming into its own in a time when there is significant attention paid to the medicalized body. To an extent never before, medicine can both test our blood for rare diseases and make predictions for our children based on the most minute aspects of our genes. Of course, it is no secret that sperm counts are falling worldwide, most likely due to the environmental toxins spewed into every facet of our lives by the relentless pursuit of profit.

If there is a liberating level to the options sperm donation provides us, it is the idea of conception without sex. I am not talking about an "immaculate" conception, but the potential for conception without a live penis. This option is now available, not only to married, monogamous couples who want to bear their own children without an outsider's penis entering into the relationship (which usually only happens with adultery), but also to single and lesbian mothers. That is the most rewarding part of my work, to create more options for loving parents of all genders and sexual orientations to bring children into the world. Love, not genetics, makes a family, and it is very heartwarming to hear the stories of parents for whom donor insemination helped create their family. I can only hope that the recipients of my sperm have the values of my personal friends who have used sperm donors and are not snobs, racists, prudish rich people, or child abusers. Someday I imagine I will have friends in need of a sperm donor, and I will be able to provide sperm for them, knowing the child will grow up in a wonderful family. That would truly be sperm donation for love instead of for money.

But for now, I'm in it for the money. As the owner of a penis but not a womb, I am more invested in being male than ever. Never one to care much about gender, suddenly I am able to use my testicles to turn a buck. That's an incredibly empowering feeling. But like many jobs in this society of temp workers, there are no guarantees, no health benefits, no plan for the future.

In the final analysis, it's quite rewarding to be paid fifty dollars to play with myself. But while I am paid for my sperm, they also take blood and urine at will, and I've been hired mostly because of my genetic characteristics, while others will be rejected on that basis. Like any job these days, it has significant problems, but at least it helps me buy my survival without selling too much of my time.

22

Orange Phone

Laurie Sirois

I found a company in *The Yellow Pages,* called them up, and went to their downtown office for an interview, which was actually a form-filling session and a rundown of time sheet and log-on procedures. I already had the job, based on my initial phone voice, I guessed. The place was called Orange Phone, and the time sheets were pale orange. I was to work from home, logging on whenever I liked via the telephone keypad and marking the calls I got on the time sheets—but I'm not sure why, as calls were logged by the computer as well. I couldn't lie. I had to record a ten-second intro that would play in a menu of girls' voices for the callers, who would choose their favorite one before punching in credit card informa- tion. If it cleared, the call would be forwarded to that woman's house and would begin.

My instructions were to get a guy off in no less than four min- utes, and no more than fifteen. For any time amount within that range, I got paid four dollars. That was it: four dollars a call. If the guy wasn't "done" at fifteen minutes, it was my job to cut him off and make him call back if he wanted more. (If I went over fifteen minutes, it didn't matter; I still only got four dollars.) So I would lie and say, "The computer's going to cut us off," at around fourteen and a half minutes and then just hang up in the middle of a sentence. I loved that, cutting off my own moans. It was my favorite part. "Oh, oh baby, you—" I figured if I got four calls an hour, it was double the wage of my day job. But for sex work, it was nothing. And, of course, because I had to be at home and wait for calls, it was hard to do anything else. So I didn't log on very often. The biggest check I ever got was for about eighty dollars: pathetic.

Somehow, I developed interactions with a few regulars who'd find me whenever I was on. I'd had fun recording my message: "Hi, I'm Eve. Tell me your fantasies, and I'd love to indulge you." My voice was deeper than the other girls' and my hope was to stick out from the crowd. There were usually only eight to ten girls logged on at a time. When I'd get a call, I had the choice to accept it or not. But there was this whole list of penalties—if I refused a call when I was logged on, I'd get docked one dollar. Or, if a call was less than four minutes, same thing.

I almost always accepted calls, and this was my approach: we'd do introductions, during which I was generally asked what I was wearing and what I looked like. I'd make some shit up, depending on my mood, though usually I was the black-haired girl in nothing but underwear, touching myself. Then I'd say, "What's your fanta-seeeee . . ." It was easier to work with whatever idea they already had in their heads than to make something up. A lot of times, the guy would do most of the talking, and I would moan and sigh. Real easy. I was never really naked or touching myself, though occasionally I'd get turned on. (At that point in my life, this disturbed me. Now, it wouldn't.)

I had one guy named John who would call me over and over for up to an hour at a time. He was great: he'd have a porno on his TV and tell me he was a director who traveled the states making them. He'd call me from "Atlanta," "Dallas," "Denver." He was probably just a businessman. But he'd say, "Listen to this scene. Can you hear it?" (I barely could.) "This is my favorite. I directed it; this actress is hot. Can you hear her? Does she sound hot?" and I'd moan and say, "Yeah, she's really hot. I love to listen to her," and wouldn't have to say anything else for a couple minutes while he got it on with himself and his pay per view. But he couldn't get off unless I was on the phone with him. The voyeur needed a voyeur.

I heard from several men who picked my voice because I sounded bisexual. They all then arrived at the conclusion that I was willing to fuck them up the ass with a dildo. This dumbfounded me. Really, several guys made the leap from my voice to the dildo, all in their separate worlds, a synchronicity of thought. It was amazing, and I would fuck them all. A few men would also ask for my home number. A common misconception among johns was that what I really wanted was a boyfriend and not the money. One guy, Steve, would want me to talk him through jerking off, and I would dance with him around his cock, make him travel up the back of it slowly, make him thrust with his hips, then linger at the tip, then jerk up and down, up and down the shaft and he'd say, "You're really good at this. You sound like you have one of your own. Are you sure you don't have one of your own? You really know what you're doing."

One day I accepted a call from a person with a severe stutter. His name—I eventually got—was Jimmy. "I-I-I-I l-live . . . with m-my p-p-p-parents." He said, "I-I'm . . . s-s-slow." We had a little get-to-know-each-other session, and I figured out that he was almost forty and lived in southern California. He wanted to know what I really did for a living, and by the time he got to that question, I had such a soft spot for him I wanted to tell him. I wanted to tell him I was a kid in San Francisco, trying to create my own life, but struggling with being poor. . . . But it was better to uphold the fantasy, I think, that I was just there for the callers' needs and that I waited for them and loved it.

Jimmy became a regular. It was great because his language challenge drew the calls out, and he'd call back three, four times in a session. He started to tell me more and more about his life. "My . . . b-b-b-broth-th-ther b-b-b-beats me . . . i-in th-th-th-th-the b-back . . . yard. . . . I-I-I-I'm worth . . . less. H-he kn-knows it." I was not able to hide my own concern, but I didn't want to play therapist, either, so I said, more cheerleader-like than parental, "You're not worthless! You're great!" And he'd reply, "N-no. I l-l-l-like it." I was starting to understand. "It t-t-turns me on."

Jimmy wanted me to abuse him too. After we'd established a certain level of trust, he asked me to tell him to do things. "What kind of things, Jimmy?" "I-I-I w-want to h-hurt m-m-m-m-myself." I was eighteen. I had a hard time being a creative S/M top, let alone knowing his situation. But he was paying me. "And . . . s-s-s-s-silly th-things. I-I-I-I-I c-c-can do s-s-s-s-silly th-things." "Okay, Jimmy, cluck like a chicken." "Wh-what?" I could hear in his words that he was smiling. "Cluck like a chicken, and jump around the room. You're a chicken." He put the phone down, slowly, and did it. I could hear stuttered clucks approach and recede, and it broke my heart. When he got back, he said, "I-I ha-have a ha-hard-on."

"Touch yourself," I said. "I want you to touch yourself and cluck like a chicken. Keep clucking." This was a successful session. He had what sounded like a great orgasm, with these stuttered clucks. I almost cried.

Jimmy kept calling back, week after week, and it got more and more difficult for me. I'd make him tie fabric around his wrist until his hand turned blue, while he was jerking off. Or I'd make him slap himself. Or hold his breath. I was running out of ideas. I'd make him jerk off until he almost came, then make him stop and wait. He loved that one. His stuttering would get excited and almost fluid.

"E-eeeve. I h-h-h—have t-to a-a-ask you s-s-s-s-s-some . . . th-th-thing," Jimmy said one day, as soon as I answered the call. "Go ahead!" I replied. "W-w-w-will you t-t-t-tell m-me how to k-kill my-s-s-self??" He was quiet, waiting for me to respond. "Jimmy, are you serious?" P-p-p-please . . . p-p-p-lease," he began to beg. *Was* he serious? Was this a fantasy of autoerotic asphyxiation? More of the self-punishment vibe? "P-p-p-p-p-please." "Jimmy, I don't want to do that. Let's do something else. Do you have a fantasy?" I asked. "I-I t-told y-you," he replied. That was his fantasy, but where was the line between a story and reality? I tried to soften the wish, and told him to place his head under a pillow while he jerked off, knowing that as long as he could talk to me he was getting air. But he was persistent. "I c-c-c-could j-j-jump o-o-o-out th-the win-d-d-dow. I h-h-h-hate m-my f-f-f-f-family. P-p-p-please. T-tell me to j-j-jump."

How long had Jimmy had this fantasy? I tried to talk around it, but he called back several times in succession, and it became clear that he was fixated on wanting to jump. I was getting paid. Was this my job? Would verbalizing the command just give him a huge instant orgasm? Or would he jump out the window? I couldn't take the risk that he would actually do it. I just wanted to get him off at this point, I really did, and I was attached to him. "Jimmy. I'm sorry." "Wh-wh-what!" He said. He knew what was coming. "I'm sorry. I can't do it." I thought about making him call 911, encouraging him to leave his family and live on his own, telling him that he was valuable and that his life was worth having. "I'm sorry, Jimmy," I said again. "B-b-bye," he stammered, sadly, and I hung up. He never called again.

-23-

Outreach

Justice

Sometimes when I go out to hand out condoms, I run into people who want to pay me for sex, so I end up going with them. I'm supposed to be standing on the street corner, acting nice and giving out my condoms, and, instead, I'm having sex with tricks. I reach out to them in their cars.

I have a lot of fun when I'm doing my outreach because I make it fun. I don't go out to look for tricks, but, most times, they'll come my way when I least expect it. I'll go out expecting just to do my outreach and get it over with, and I'll end up meeting someone and going out with them and having fun, partying, and making some money.

I met my lover while I was prostituting. I used to do outreach and have a boyfriend and prostitute at the same time; that's how I got into a lot of trouble. I used to go out sometimes: I'd say, "I'll be back," and my boyfriend wouldn't see me for two or three days. He used to lose his mind; he'd ask, "How could you do that to me? I can't keep going through this. I can't eat. I can't sleep," and it got to the point where I used to do it intentionally to make him suffer and test his love. Then I started seeing how he was losing weight—he'd always been built, and from the neck down, he started looking skinny. So I stopped going out and not coming back because I realized that some part of him really did go out to me.

It was hard for me to stop tricking because the money was so good. But I couldn't be with my boyfriend at the same time. He didn't like the idea of me prostituting at all. It got to the point where he became really violent. He didn't even want me to do outreach because when I did outreach, I didn't come back.

That was always my excuse: I'd say, "I want to do outreach. I'll be back later." Then bright and early in the morning, I'd rush home. I stopped prostituting, and I was just doing outreach to people in my neighborhood, people practically right outside my door. Because my boyfriend didn't want me meeting people. He was overprotective of me, really obsessed with me.

He broke my arm because I was ten minutes late meeting him and I'd been with a john. We were supposed to go to Florida that morning on Amtrak; we had forty minutes to get there, and we were supposed to be there an hour early. I told him we could rush there, but he couldn't accept that. He'd had his mind set on getting to Florida and laughing in people's faces. I'd caught him cheating on me, for eight months, and people said we weren't going to make it.

When I turned the corner to go downstairs and get our luggage, he just started hitting me. We were in the basement, and he beat me to the point where I felt a break in my arm. I couldn't lift anything. He said take all the luggage and put it in a shopping cart. So I had to do that with a broken arm. He kept hitting me and telling me to shut up. He had a bad temper, and I knew that, but I kept with him, hoping that one day he'd break out of it. But it was still in him, all that rage that he felt. We tried to work on it, talked about it all the time.

I think he felt betrayed or crossed, and he took it out on me. I still talk to him, but I fear for my life, and I tell him that. I tried to break up with him just yesterday. He's in jail now. I said, "I can't guarantee that when you get out of jail, that I'll wait for you. Because you hurt me." He said, "Well, we hurt each other." I said, "This time, it's something that I have to live with every day; my arm might never be the same again. I'm scared of you." He started begging; he said, "It's never going to happen again," and I said, "That's what you said the first time, when you busted my whole eye open."

He always wanted me to go home to my father, but I don't want to be told by someone else, "You've got to be home by twelve o'clock." I say God bless the child that's got his own: that's me. Every day's a struggle, to try to pay rent and the bills, and I kinda get a rush out of that. I don't like living dangerous, but it's being responsible; it's life. He can't accept that. He feels like someone or something or society owes him because they took so many years away from him; he was seventeen years old when he went to jail for eleven years for murder, then he got out of jail and fell in love with me. Now—six years later—I want to leave him. I say to myself there's got to be something better. I don't want to get hurt or killed.

He said he's crazy about me. So crazy about me that he broke my arm—I just got the cast off yesterday. I had the cast on for eight weeks. That was the fourth time in six years that he abused me physically. In one way or another, it usually had something to do with outreach.

Luck

Sarah Fran Wisby

Sometimes I feel like luck made flesh, the lady they pray to and pray for. They come to me, furtive and bold and hollow and burning, and they leave coddled and sated, a little poorer, but they've tapped some of my wealth too.

They come in broad daylight. I envy them stepping out of bright cars onto sun-crazed cement, the money carefully folded in their pockets. I watch through the peephole, size them up. My hands and feet are cold, but I look smashing in a fourteen-dollar dress, ice blonde hair, purple lips, and frosty blue eyeshadow; my only visible flaw is the bruise on my leg where the dog bit, before I taught her gentleness.

I envy their mobility, the ease with which they pursue their satisfaction. The fact that places like this exist for them, women like me sit by telephones waiting for their calls. There is a marketplace for their urges. If only my half of the story were so simple.

I'd like it to be peachy all the time. I'd like it to be erotic and unabashed. I'd like to tell you their come smells like sweet cream and their fingers click inside me like brilliant keys, unlocking my never-ending orgasms. Or else I'd like to tell you I never touch the stuff, don't trust them as far as I can blow them, and that if they mess with me, I shoot them right between the eyes with the semi-automatic I keep tucked in my cleavage for such purposes.

There's a line I walk between disdain and unconditional love, a watery line I can't always focus on. Sometimes, in midsession, my own desire falls out of me like shoplifted goods at the grocery store and the client becomes the bewildered clerk, unsure if he should report me or let me go. Humiliation gets me even hotter, and my own fantasies flash on like TV. In the fantasies, it's a girl pretending to be a trick and I'm pretending to be a whore—isn't that funny? My moans get loud and hyper-real; I decide to go for it. I'll work through a heavy orgasm with some man who looks at me like I'm the prettiest thing he's ever laid eyes on or maybe he doesn't even notice I came too, but we'll hold each other soft and sticky and I won't be sad the way I get with girls. I'll still be me and strong in my own skin and glad he doesn't know my real name.

Contributors

D-L Alvarez was born in Stockton, California, to biker parents Sharkie and Ethel. He has traveled widely and has lived (since age eighteen) in Colorado, Paris, Berlin, San Francisco, and Brooklyn, NY. Some of his short stories have appeared in print previously, but this is his first autobiographical work. He'd like to thank Mistress Josephine, who taught him plenty and helped him get started in the pro-dom business.

Christopher Boyd is a writer and filmmaker living in Florida. A graduate of New York University, he recently worked with the documentary unit at ABC News in New York. His film on the sex industry, *Private Shows*, has been seen in venues from Los Angeles to London. He is currently writing his first novel.

Coffee lives in New York.

Alvin Eros has appeared in some two dozen adult videos and worked as a stripper for longer than he cares to admit. He advises aspiring sex workers not to go into the life without seeing the movies *Gypsy* and *Sweet Charity*. He is a California native.

Eileen Geoghegan "turned herself out" in 1976. Her early career as a sex worker occurred in a world now beyond the imagination—before AIDS. "A Slice of 'The Life'" is the centerpiece of her memoir, *QUAKE*. It began as a "recovery" exercise, highlighting prostitution as pathology. She decided to salvage the intentions with which she undertook these adventures—the fun, fear, humor, and heroin—in writing classes as she pursued her BA in English. After she received her MA in Theological Studies, the work became an alternative spiritual autobiography—an episode in her continuing search for transcendent experience.

Nina Hartley, RN, is a sixteen-year veteran of adult videos. She is a dancer, an educator, a director, an actress, an advocate, an activist, a writer, and a swinger. One of the most vocal of the sex-positive feminists who came on the scene in the mid-1980s, she is tireless in promoting her sexual philosophy, a unique synthesis of science, humanism, feminism, socialism, and personal responsibility. A charismatic and engaging speaker, she is popular with a wide range of audiences. She is at her best when defending her profession to the world, using her fame effectively when speaking to the public. After starting as a dancer while going to nursing school, Hartley found she liked the explicit medium enough to make the transition to a photographic record. In 1985, after graduating magna cum laude, she went full-time into the movies. Winner of most of porndom's most prestigious awards, at this stage in her career, Hartley continues to act, as well as produce, direct, and write her own videos. She lives with her husband, Dave, and her wife, Bobby, in a long-standing ménage à trois. They, along with their two cats, live in Nina's hometown of Berkeley, California.

Jo Anne C. Heen worked in porn retail for five years. She left after being shot during a robbery. She now works as a customer service rep in a secured building.

Justice lives in New York.

Kowalski is a writer, performer, visual artist, and sex worker living in San Francisco. He has performed "Joel" (under the title *Prostitute, Therapist, Babysitter, Priest*) in Chicago, San Francisco, and Santa Monica. He has a BFA in filmmaking from the University of Wisconsin, Milwaukee. He has been working in collage for ten years and has shown his work in Los Angeles, Chicago, and San Francisco. His work creates erotic "religious" icons from appropriated images considered pornographic. He has work in private collections throughout the country and in the permanent collection of the Tom of Finland Foundation. He bases his sex work practice on the belief that touch and intimacy have the ability to transform, heal, and promote change, in both his clients and himself. Through both sex work and art, he continues to aspire to higher levels of shamelessness.

Mariah lives in New York.

Vernon Maulsby (Mikki) is a forty-one-year-old pre-op TS who is also a published poet/writer/playwright, as well as a newly self-initiated Wiccan. Mikki is addicted to the printed word and sees herself as a princess trapped in the body of a mangy old bear. Her hobbies include art, bookbinding, and music. She doesn't suffer fools easily and is currently in prison.

Jill Nagle is the editor of *Whores and Other Feminists* (1997) and associate editor of *Male Lust: Pleasure, Power, and Transformation* (2000). Her work has appeared in the anthologies *Looking Queer*, *PoMoSexuals, First Person Sexual, Bisexual Politics*, and *Closer to Home*, as well as in such periodicals as *Girlfriends, Black Sheets*, and *Anything That Moves*. Her latest book is *The Female Fag* (2000).

Scott "Spunk" O'Hara (1961-1998) was a well-known porn star who appeared in twenty-six films between 1983 and 1992. He was editor and publisher of the sex journal *STEAM* ("the literate queer's guide to sex and controversy") from 1993 to 1996 and was published in numerous anthologies, magazines, and newspapers. His first book of short stories, *Do-It-Yourself Piston Polishing (for Non-Mechanics)*, was released in August 1996. His autobiography, *Autopornography: A Memoir of Life in the Lust Lane*, was published in 1997. He is also the author of a posthumously published book, *Rarely Pure and Never Simple: Selected Essays of Scott O'Hara* (1999). Scott died of AIDS-related complications in February 1998.

Eva Pendleton is a writer and retired sex worker. She is a member of the Dangerous Bedfellows Collective and a co-editor of *Policing Public Sex: Queer Politics and the Future of AIDS Activism* (1996).

Brian Pera lives in Memphis, Tennessee. His first novel, *Troublemaker*, is forthcoming in spring 2000.

David Porter, through biotechnology, hopes one day to have hot sex with a genetic clone of himself. It is not a fantasy of narcissistic self-love, but rather a gene fetish. He hopes to obtain a patent on his body and sell it as cyborgware to the uninitiated.

Carol Queen has a doctorate in sexology, though she got no extra credit for being a whore. How unfair is that?! She blames prostitution for getting her started on her writing career. She is the author of *Real Live Nude Girl: Chronicles of Sex-Positive Culture; The Leather Daddy and the Femme; Exhibitionism for the Shy;* and co-editor, with Lawrence Schimel, of *PoMoSexuals: Challenging Assumptions About Gender and Sexuality* (winner of a Lambda Literary Award in 1998); *Switch Hitters: Lesbians Write Gay Male Erotica and Gay Men Write Lesbian Erotica* (also with Schimel); and *Sex Spoken Here: Stories from the Good Vibrations Reading Circle* (with Jack Davis). Her Web address is <www.carolqueen.com> and she writes regularly for *Playboy Online.*

Ann Renee performs and publishes her autobiographical stories. Co-founder of Abundant Fuck Publications out of San Francisco and member of The Moon Has Fat Thighs theater collective, Ann's most recent publications include an essay in *Whores and Other Feminists.* She's currently working on an autobiographical book titled *The Phoenix Wants Me.*

Gary Rosen is a writer and troublemaker whose heroes include Todd Haynes, Scott Heim, Dennis Cooper, Sam D'Allessandro, Stephen Beachy, Karl Soehnlein, Michelle Tea, and Herve Guibert. He currently lives in New York City but has been eyeballing Los Angeles. His e-mail address is <warpdrive@hotmail.com>.

Faye Rowland, born too many years ago, has lived in most of the fifty states and five countries. With eighteen years of education, she still can't get a decent job. With fourteen years of military service, two years of "sex service," and many years of service sector "service"—she (formerly "he") was ready, by 1988, to switch genders. All considered, she's the quintessentially unemployable, white-trash, rock-and-roll refugee that so threatens Western civilization. She also paints in her spare time.

Laurie Sirois lives and works in San Francisco but is soon to make the Great Escape. She does photography and film, writes, sings, and currently works in technology. Stay tuned for a screenplay.

Isadora Stern lives in New York.

Tony Valenzuela is a writer, activist, and sex worker based in Los Angeles. He has been published in *Genre, Gay and Lesbian Times, POZ*, and *GCN*. He has also been featured in dozens of publications for his work in AIDS activism and sexual liberation organizing, including *Out, POZ, The Advocate, Skinflicks*, and *LA Weekly*. He is currently working on a solo performance piece.

Sarah Fran Wisby is a writer and a sensual masseuse. Her writing has appeared in *Best Lesbian Erotica 1999* and in *On Our Backs*. She is the author of the chapbook *Ambulance in a Traffic Jam*.

Order Your Own Copy of
This Important Book for Your Personal Library!

TRICKS AND TREATS
Sex Workers Write About Their Clients

_____in hardbound at $39.95 (ISBN: 0-7890-0703-7)

_____in softbound at $17.95 (ISBN: 1-56023-162-9)

COST OF BOOKS_____

OUTSIDE USA/CANADA/
MEXICO: ADD 20%_____

POSTAGE & HANDLING_____
*(US: $3.00 for first book & $1.25
for each additional book)
Outside US: $4.75 for first book
& $1.75 for each additional book)*

SUBTOTAL_____

IN CANADA: ADD 7% GST_____

STATE TAX_____
*(NY, OH & MN residents, please
add appropriate local sales tax)*

FINAL TOTAL_____
*(If paying in Canadian funds,
convert using the current
exchange rate. UNESCO
coupons welcome.)*

☐ **BILL ME LATER:** ($5 service charge will be added)
(Bill-me option is good on US/Canada/Mexico orders only;
not good to jobbers, wholesalers, or subscription agencies.)

☐ Check here if billing address is different from
shipping address and attach purchase order and
billing address information.

Signature_____

☐ **PAYMENT ENCLOSED: $**_____

☐ **PLEASE CHARGE TO MY CREDIT CARD.**

☐ Visa   ☐ MasterCard   ☐ AmEx   ☐ Discover
☐ Diner's Club

Account #_____

Exp. Date_____

Signature_____

Prices in US dollars and subject to change without notice.

NAME _____

INSTITUTION _____

ADDRESS _____

CITY _____

STATE/ZIP _____

COUNTRY _____ COUNTY (NY residents only) _____

TEL _____ FAX _____

E-MAIL_____
May we use your e-mail address for confirmations and other types of information? ☐ Yes   ☐ No

Order From Your Local Bookstore or Directly From
The Haworth Press, Inc.
10 Alice Street, Binghamton, New York 13904-1580 • USA
TELEPHONE: 1-800-HAWORTH (1-800-429-6784) / Outside US/Canada: (607) 722-5857
FAX: 1-800-895-0582 / Outside US/Canada: (607) 772-6362
E-mail: getinfo@haworthpressinc.com
PLEASE PHOTOCOPY THIS FORM FOR YOUR PERSONAL USE.

BOF96